T0208525

Defining Faith

Definition Series – Volume 2

NANETTE T. FRIEND

authorHOUSE

AuthorHouse™
1663 Liberty Drive
Bloomington, IN 47403
www.authorhouse.com
Phone: 833-262-8899

Published by AuthorHouse   12/13/2021

ISBN: 978-1-6655-4504-4 (sc)
ISBN: 978-1-6655-4505-1 (e)

Library of Congress Control Number: 2019912165

Print information available on the last page.

This is a true account of my journey while incarcerated within a women's
state prison. However, please understand that most all of the names and
locations within this account have been changed to protect the innocent
and very sensitive nature of the stories portrayed within the series.

Endorsements

n. the act or process of endorsing; something that is written in the process of endorsing; an indication that someone or something is favorable, acceptable, or satisfactory.

"Amidst the fears, tears, shame, heartaches, frustrations, longings, hopes, and dreams which comprise life in prison, I felt like I was right there with her! What a wonderful story of redemption and salvation which easily could be anyone's story. Well done!"

~ *Jack Stockdale*
Pastor/Church Planter/Foreign Missionary
New Song Community Church, Reynoldsburg, OH

"Nanette has learned from first-hand experience what it means to have Proverbs 3:5-6 activated in her life. She has recorded this portion of her life with humility, honesty, and love. She has walked through the fire and come out with the fragrance of Jesus on her life. It is with great honor that I recommend her book, "Defining Faith".

~ *Lois A. Hoshor*
Evangelist/Author
Soul Seekers Evangelistic Association

Trust in the LORD with all your heart and lean not on your own understanding; in all your ways submit to him, and he will make your paths straight.　　　　　　*Proverbs 3:5-6*

DEDICATION

n: The act of dedicating; the state of being dedicated to (an event, project, time, etc.); a formal, printed inscription in a book, piece of music, etc. dedicating it to a person, cause, or the like.

In loving dedication to my precious Mother: as in any family, there were many years of fond memories and celebrations, as well as painful episodes within our lives. My heart thrived with the unwavering love, commitment, and deep *faith* you undeniably portrayed to each of your eight children and countless grandchildren. This was never more prominent than during the devastating loss and pre-mature death of three of those children; as well as the loss of your husband to whom you devoted your life and love.

As a young child, I well remember climbing up beside you in your sizeable bed to watch numerous black and white movies of the "Greatest Stories of the Bible." Even then I could sense your search for hope, deep conviction, genuine love and total devotion to a God who would provide you with enduring protection, purpose and promise.

I pray there is finally eternal rest for your soul, Mom. A small woman, yet a mighty force; there has never been a question of the inner strength and devotion you have revealed to anyone who has ever known and loved you. I miss you terribly.

Contents

n: The individual items or topics that are dealt with in a publication or document; the material, including text and images that constitutes a publication or document; the substantive or meaningful part; the meaning or significance of a literary or artistic work.

Introduction

n: Formal personal presentation; preliminary part leading to the main part; something introduced.

*"Truly I tell you, if you have **faith** as small as a mustard seed, you can say to this mountain, 'Move from here to there,' and it will move. Nothing will be impossible for you."*
Matthew 17:20

Defining . . .

n: The act of defining, distinct or clarify; clear; the formal statement of the meaning or significance of the word, phrase; the accuracy of sound or picture reproduction; degree of clarity; statement conveying fundamental character.

. . . Faith

n: Allegiance to duty or a person: loyalty; fidelity to one's promises; sincerity of intentions acted in good faith; belief and trust in and loyalty to God.; belief in the traditional doctrines of a religion; firm belief in something for which there is no proof. Something that is believed, especially with strong conviction; complete trust.

As I continue in my attempt to clarify each segment with a definition of the main theme for the chapter throughout each and every book, please remember that my true desire is only to draw attention to and leave no uncertainty regarding the nature of each subject, and what it will portray.

Teach me your way, LORD, that I may rely on your faithfulness; give me an undivided heart, that I may fear your name.   Psalm 86:11

Many of you have inquired repeatedly when this edition of the series would be complete. For this, I thank you for your continued encouragement, patience, and ***faith*** (loyalty to one's promises).

Please know that each of you have been on my heart . . . and understanding that this has been a very hard year for everyone, I initially believed it would undoubtedly give me the time needed to concentrate on this second edition of the series. However, within a few weeks after publication of my first book, ***Defining Truth***, my mother suffered a massive stroke and needed to be cared for. Soon after, she was moved to a nursing/rehabilitation center close to my home. Throughout the following months, it became evident Mom was most likely drawing near to her final season with us, and I found myself trying to spend extra time with her. The onset of COVID-19 in February of 2020, shut the facility down and we were no longer permitted to visit anymore. Within weeks, the nurses called to report that Mom was severely depressed, wouldn't eat or drink anything, and couldn't understand why her children would not come to see her, or pick her up to take her home. (Mom suffered from dementia.) I couldn't bear it anymore. My siblings and I decided she needed to come home with me. We enjoyed and cherished the remaining months we had left with Mom until she slipped into the arms of Jesus just after Mother's Day of that year.

Later that summer and into the fall, I became immobile

with severe hip, back, and leg pain and numbness, and found that I could barely sleep at night, let alone try to walk or sit in a chair. I also developed carpal tunnel and couldn't write, use the computer, or perform other daily activities. I knew that I knew that Satan was attacking me, but I couldn't and wouldn't give up. My heart ached to write and provide the testimony that God had placed upon my heart to share with you. I prayed, cried, and pleaded with God harder than I had in a very long time - for complete healing, comfort, and the ability to once again be able to write. I longed for the tranquility that I found in my writing, and spending time with the Lord.

Within a few more months, we learned my husband has been suffering from a terminal illness, and all of the doubt, fear, questions and uncertainty of my life took yet another turn. I felt as though I was paralyzed with disbelief and fear of what God truly had planned for our life. I wasn't sure I could function anymore. How could I possibly go on without my husband, the love of my life, and best friend? We were forced to face this together, and our marriage would be tried to an extent we had never encountered before.

Please know, however, that to this very day, God has not only healed me, strengthened me, and brought my husband and I closer together than we have ever been - but Dan has also found his trust, *faith* and salvation in God like never before. Throughout his continued suffering, countless tests, blood work, biopsies, and appointments each week - Dan continues to work as he can. We have realized that only though faith, are we able to truly love each other with a new appreciation of our life together.

Needless to say, I have found my way back to writing

and the healing of my heart. So, to catch you up – in my first book, I had taken you through the first seven weeks of my perilous journey while incarcerated within a woman's state prison. Throughout that time, I was indeed, searching for and determined to find the very essence of "truth." It was not until this part of my story, however, that I actually understand and *accept* the "truth": the salvation of our Lord and Savior, Jesus Christ! Please know however, that I would soon realize it would only be through my search for *faith*: the *confidence* and *hope* of things unseen, that I would continue to honestly seek, and fully accept God into my life, and into my heart.

This is the continuing true account of my journey while still incarcerated. However, I have now left the main facility of the State Reformatory for Women - and in the process of traveling to a minimum-security Women's State Prison. Several of the names and locations have been changed to protect the innocent (as well as the guilty) and sensitive nature of the stories portrayed within the series. Let there be no mistake, however, that regardless of the stories revealed; or of the testimony portrayed within the pages of this manuscript; the only true definition I wish to convey without question is the understanding and defining clarity of the Truth, **Faith,** Hope, Love, Forgiveness, and Promise of our Savior Jesus Christ. This second book will continue the story, illustrating the *faith* I would come to understand within my life, as well as my new and continued walk with God throughout those months.

Join me now on my search for *Faith. God Bless!*

Know therefore that the LORD *your God is God; he is*

*a **faithful** God, keeping his covenant of love to a thousand generations of those who love him and keep his commandments.*

Deuteronomy 7:9

CHAPTER 1

✍ *Association* ✍

n: an organization of people with common purpose, having formal structure; friendship, companionship, connections, combination or relation of ideas, feelings, etc.; perception, reasoning: an idea, image, feeling, etc.; alliance, union, society, company, fellowship.

Then the high priest and all his associates, who were members of the party of the Sadducees [a sect or group of Jews that fulfilled various political, social, and religious roles] *were filled with jealousy. They arrested the apostles and put them in the public jail. But during the night an angel of the Lord opened the doors of the jail and brought them out. "Go, stand in the temple courts," he said, "and tell the people all about this new life."* Acts 5:17-20

Seated in the third row directly behind the bus driver, my nose pressed firmly against the icy window; I peered at the streets, the early morning lights of the city just waking up, and the congested traffic of cars filled with people on their way to work, school or appointments at this very early hour. I raised my hands, firmly secured with cold metal handcuffs, upward in an attempt to scrape the crust of thin ice off the panes; as well as to erase the steam I had created on the glass with my breath. Once again, I could feel the pain of the handcuffs tightening deep into my flesh. And yet, I didn't care. On the other side of those glass windows was freedom; the freedom I so longed for and had taken for granted. People listening to their car radios for the news events unfolding that day, the weather forecast, early morning talk-show hosts telling jokes; or possibly listening to top hits by Phil Collins, Britney Spears or Whitney Houston. A construction worker sipping his hot-steaming coffee, a bank teller applying lipstick in the rear-view mirror, or a gentleman checking if he'd shaved close enough that morning. People discussing last minute appointments, plans of the day with their children, spouses, or co-workers on their push-button mobile phones of the late nineties.

Do they truly have any understanding or appreciation of the independence and freedom they have? I somberly thought to myself.

I suddenly realized I no longer had any association with this group of people; nor did I belong to this community of individuals who would routinely commute back and forth to work every single day, and most likely complain about it the entire time. Only a few months prior, I remembered being disgruntled with the traffic, the weather, the long drive, the rising cost of gasoline to travel to work each day; as well as the cold early morning hours when I would much rather still be at home in my bed all wrapped up in a nice warm blanket. I had taken so many things for granted, but now longed to once again be included among these commuters freely enroute to their destinations that morning.

What had happened to this small-town country girl from the Midwest who had hopes and dreams of becoming someone of distinction and success? The second oldest of eight children, my lofty dreams of going to college and traveling, an idyllic marriage with several up-and-coming children . . . was just that . . . a dream. I had always worked hard helping my mother with everything required of me at home, including the care of my younger siblings. My very first job was in the dining halls of the local liberal arts college when I was 15-years old. Raised within this village of a college-oriented population, and always a fairly good student, I was a member of the (GAA) Girls Athletic Association, the school band, Science club, French club, Y-teens, Girl Scouts and 4-H clubs. I never stopped longing for something more than our simple and hard life at the Braxton household located on the outskirts of town.

I was devastated as a young teenager to learn that my father would never consider allowing me to attend college, and that he portrayed my biggest and most ultimate accomplishment in life would be marriage - complete with a huge and beautiful wedding day! I was told it would then be the responsibility of my husband to support me, and that I needed to understand that my "place" as a woman was to bear and raise children, keep a clean house, and take care of my husband. I was heartbroken. I really did not want to be the stay-at-home Mom, confined and conformed to the house, yardwork, gardening, sewing, and cooking as my mother had been. I never really saw my mother resting or enjoying herself. Regardless of my father's resolve, 14 years and four children later, my marriage had terminated in divorce; and I found myself a single Mom, tirelessly struggling to make ends meet.

By now we had nearly completed the hour-long drive from the Women's State Reformatory in Maryswood and had entered into the city limits of the Pre-Release Center

(PRC) where I would now serve the remainder of my mandated year-long sentence. Having already completed seven dreadful weeks at the main prison, I was humbled and grateful to have been granted the opportunity to be transferred to the PRC, which was located so much closer to home. Still very much a women's state lockdown prison, this was a minimum-security facility designed to reform those who had less than two years remaining to serve and were now eligible to attend the programs available to them. Not to be confused with a halfway house, the intent of this secured Center was designed to prepare inmates to enter back into society.

As the morning sun was just beginning to make its presence known to the world that early frigid day in the first week of December, it was difficult to discern the layout of the compound through the dense and misty fog as we drew closer to the facility. As the prison van cautiously turned onto the icy road leading into the institution, it was clear, however, there were high metal fences with huge strands of barbed wire wrapped all along the top of the secure barricade, and giant beaming lights surrounding the exterior of the buildings and fencing.

Although dreading the unknowns of this new facility, I took a deep breath and thanked God for the opportunity to escape the constant fear and worry of being detained at Maryswood, and to leave behind the very real and deadly threats and harm. The main women's penitentiary was indeed *no joke!* I had no desire to be associated with, have connections to, or be in alliance with any of those still at Maryswood. I desperately needed to go forward in my search for clarity and redemption.

I tried to stay calm as we drew closer to the building. I could feel my heart beating faster within the cavity of my chest, in dread and anticipation of this unknown territory. A few of the women at Maryswood who had previously served time at PRC, explained I would be assigned to a room (cell) with 3 other inmates.

During the ride I asked God if I could please be placed with "good" roommates . . .

Oh, and God? If we should truly have our own rooms with roommates, could I please be assigned with those who read the Bible and don't swear all the time?

What? I had actually surprised myself at this very explicit request - although reasoned this thinking could possibly ensure my safety and sanity in this new and unfamiliar facility. However, just as quickly, I was brought back to reality as I recalled in my head the constant brutal language of the majority of inmates, especially of those who suffered from the profound need to prove their *street smart* and *tough as nails* "survival" personality.

I could only surmise – *Ok, like that was ever going to happen!*

Intake

Enter through the narrow gate. For wide is the gate and broad is the road that leads to destruction, and many enter through it.   *Matthew 7:13*

The prison van now parked at the main gate, we sat for what seemed like hours as we waited for the officers to complete a rigorous inspection of the entire bus, both the interior and exterior of the vehicle. By this time, my wrists were in unrelenting pain.

Eventually ordered to depart the bus, we carefully made our way one-by-one down the steps, slowly trudging along in our ankle-shackles in straight-line formation upon the icy blacktop parking lot. As we entered the building and long hallway, the warm air was an overwhelming welcome of relief. Ordered to stop and line up against the wall, two CO's (Corrections Officer) approached each of us, inquired of our name and prison number, and then cautiously unshackled our hands and ankles.

"Name and number?"

"Friend, Nanette. 46134," I obediently replied.

Noticing the incredibly tight cuffs and bright red indentations around my wrists, the young, blond CO asked, "*Girl*, why didn't you say something that your cuffs were too tight?"

"They really didn't get tight until I kept rubbing my hands to stay warm," I quickly explained.

"Yep, that'll do it. You can't wiggle around in these things. They'll tighten up on you." It was such a relief to have them removed.

"Thank you" I sincerely stated as I softly rubbed and attempted to soothe the pain and discomfort of my throbbing wrists.

After roll call, and everyone now free of their shackles, we were directed into the supply room which held rows and rows of shelves filled with uniforms, blankets, linens, towels, hats, coats, boots, and many other essential items. Further instructed to report to the supply staff "trustees" (trusted prisoners) stationed behind the large counter, they would assist us with selection and distribution of the proper size khaki uniforms consisting of elastic-waist pants and matching short sleeve V-neck tops. In addition, we were issued with 3-pair of each: uniform, white cotton socks, underwear and non-underwire bras, long underwear, one-piece white sackcloth textured nightgown, towels and bed linens. We were also supplied with basic daily-needs provisions, a heavy coat, knit hat, gloves and boots. With winter now well upon us, I was truly grateful we had been allotted heavy winter wear at this location!

After instructing us to stack our newly issued items into well-organized piles behind us, the trustees were then excused from the room. Medical staff were ushered inside, and we were ordered to prepare for a full-body strip search once again (having undergone the first one when leaving Maryswood). I was astounded to say the least! *What on God's green earth could they possibly think we would be able to sneak into the jail from the maximum-security prison we just left? Maybe something that had been hidden on the bus?* I sure didn't know.

The dark-haired, older CO barked "Listen up! You know the drill! Spread out, arms-length. Eyes straight ahead at all times. Disrobe and place all clothing (one-piece orange jumpsuit for transportation, underclothing and socks) in front of you for collection. Arms up. Interlock your fingers and place your hands behind your neck. Legs in the straddle position and remain at attention until ordered otherwise."

Even while in the hospital giving birth to one of my four children, the humiliation and embarrassment of complete nudity in front of strangers was definitely not one of my favorite experiences! However, this time we were also checked for lice, rashes and skin abnormalities within our eyes, ears, hair and every conceivable part of our body with a flashlight. I suppose I should have been comforted by the fact that I received a clean bill of health. *Ugh!*

Upon complete inspection, the CO instructed: "Get dressed and remain in line until you are assigned to your trustee, who will take you to the common area for further instructions and dorm assignment."

I couldn't get dressed fast enough.

Eventually appointed to an escort, each woman in our small group grabbed our own individual laundry bag filled with newly state-issued amenities and proceeded through the hallways of the Intake Area. As our guide began the tour, we were informed this was the Administration building, the main center of the campus. Within this structure, we were directed to and walked past the commissary, library, mail room, visiting area, offices of the Warden, Records Dept., and several other staff and departments; Chapel, recreational/exercise room, and various other meeting rooms. We were then led to one of the larger meeting rooms for orientation and provided a handbook regarding the many rules and regulations, map of the compound, locations of offices and classrooms, programs available, times of meals, and other essential need-to-know information.

"You must read through your handbook in its entirety as you will be responsible to know all of the rules and regulations without question," the Sergeant instructed. She also explained that although we had been granted the privilege of being reassigned to the Pre-Release Center, this was still very much a lockdown prison, and if we violated any of the rules or laws, or caused for any breach of the regulations, we would immediately be transferred back to Maryswood. *Oh hell, no! That's not going to happen! I will not be doing anything at all to send me back to that place!* I could only think to myself.

We were also provided with information regarding the various programs available on the compound, and strongly encouraged to participate in these programs. These courses would not only help us on the outside regarding family, relationships, jobs, staying sober, setting goals, life skills, etc.; but any course we completed would be duly noted in our records, and reported to our presiding judge. I wasn't sure how any of this could possibly influence the judge to reduce my mandatory 12-month prison sentence, but anything that could make the merciless year go faster, was certainly fine with me.

Approximately 45-minutes later, and the orientation now complete, one group at a time was escorted just inside the entryway on the opposite side of the building. Standing on the thin gray indoor-outdoor carpet within the atrium, our assigned trustee continued to explain the layout of the compound, as well as additional information regarding each building.

A relatively new and modern facility, there were five housing units (dorms) placed within a large circular "cul-de-sac" formation on the grounds. All housing units were 2 stories high. Set-up counterclockwise, CFS, or Central Food Services area had its own building located next to the administration/intake facility. Immediately next door to the right, our group of 3-4 women had all been assigned to Unit #1 - the only non-smoking dorm on the compound. This unit also housed the educational offices for the Dean of the Campus University and GED Instructor, as well as the Medical Facility and staff.

The trustee continued to explain the educational and computer centers for programs dedicated to teaching *Life Skills* were available in Unit #2. There was also a beautician located within this unit with whom you could schedule an appointment for a haircut – only: no styling, dyeing or "prepping" your hair.

Unit #3 was notorious for its rough and rowdy group of hard-core women. Additional classrooms were located within this unit, as well as the Chaplain's office. There was also a program within this dorm which allowed those who qualified to participate in a training program for 2-year-old puppies, grooming them to eventually become "comfort" or "healing" dogs. Inmates who qualified and worked within this program had total responsibility and care for these puppies 24/7. Trainers would come into the compound during the week to work with the women to train these dogs to someday be a calming, therapeutic and protective partner for someone. It was calming and therapeutic for the inmates as well . . . but also a very sorrowful time once the training was completed and the puppies were removed from the compound.

Unit #4 was the only unit in which those who were participating in an intense drug-rehab program were permitted to reside. There were additional classrooms and learning centers located within this dorm as well.

Completing the full circle, Unit #5 housed the "lockdown" (or "hole") cells, as well as the offices of the Captain, Lieutenants, Sergeants, etc. Adjacent to Unit #5 was a large blacktop "walk-jog," basketball courts with bleachers, and outdoor recreation area with a few picnic tables. The prison hospital was located directly across the street. The entire facility only housed approximately 500 women, compared to well over 2,700 inmates located within Maryswood.

Room #224

Eventually escorted through glass doors outside into the cold air, down the steps, and turning to the right, we walked along the sidewalk and followed the trustee up the steps and into our assigned dorm: Unit #1. Entering the center of the room and the large circular cubicle/desk area, we couldn't help but notice the well-built, handsome and dark-haired man seated in the heart of the cubicle.

"Hey Mr. Boyd! We have some newbies coming in for you today!" the trustee cheerfully declared as she bounced into the atrium.

"Oh yeah?" Mr. Boyd readily answered. "Ok ladies, take a seat over here behind me."

With a calm and cheerful disposition, Mr. Boyd directed us to the rows of molded plastic chairs lined up in front of the TV area. We sat patiently and quietly as we observed some of the inmates watching television, using the microwave, carrying baskets of dirty clothes into the laundry room; searching for books, games or videos from the shelves of the mini-library provided within each dorm; playing cards or ping pong at the tables, using the telephones, braiding each other's hair, or just sitting and talking to each other. We would later understand that the majority of the women were either at their work location or attending classes.

After several minutes, Mr. Boyd walked around and stood before us as he instructed us regarding phone privileges, meal/count times and room regulations. He had previously summoned someone from each of the appointed rooms to accompany us to our cell, as well as to make certain we understood which bunk, drawers, closet, desk, etc. had been assigned for our use.

"Ok, you are good to go ladies!" Mr. Boyd announced. "If you have any questions at all, ask your roomie or you can speak directly with me." Surprisingly, the only real question I wanted to ask Mr. Boyd at that moment, was if he was married. I had to chuckle to myself.

"Hey, I'm Sofie. What's your name?" my delegated roomie questioned me. A large, stocky black woman, most likely in her mid-to-late thirties, Sofie had soft puffy cheeks that accentuated her dimples, small brown freckles that dotted her nose, brilliant white teeth, and a beautiful smile. Her short, dark hair was tinted with red streaks, and separated out into pigtails wrapped up with different brightly-colored rubber bands.

"Friend, Nanette." I answered.

"So, that really is your name, huh?" Sofie suspiciously inquired. "Ok, well you stick with me, and I'll watch out for you. Your name already been the topic of discussion 'round here."

Immediately, I stopped in my tracks. "What do you mean?" I could only fear the worst. Could "word" about Peaches' vendetta and death threats against me have possibly reached the Pre-Release Center from Maryswood, and now I was being stalked by some of the women here? I could hardly breathe.

"Oh, you know how people like to play. With a name like "Friend" everybody be saying 'Oooo, will she be *my* friend?' I told them they even think about playing with you, they will have me to answer to. Trust me, they all know better than to mess with me!" I was surprised that Sofie had already determined to protect me. Until that very moment, she had never met me. I wasn't quite sure how to take that. I guess I was pleased she was willing to stand up for me. *But how on earth did people know my name already?* I had to ask her.

"Oh, you be surprised what people know 'bout everything goin' on 'round here. As soon as those trustees left the stock room this morning, everybody's business out there!" she explained. *Oh, dear Lord. Please help me,* I sighed as I followed Sofie to the entrance of the stairwell leading up to the 2nd floor where our room was located.

I would soon learn that Sofie was serving ten years for 2nd degree felony arson, as well as miscellaneous theft and drug charges. She would later describe yet another incident of how she had been in a fight with an inmate and had thrown her over the top of the railings onto the 1st floor. Sofie had been returned to Maryswood, with additional time and charges added to her case for malicious battery. By this time, however, she had less than 2 years remaining of her entire sentence.

Large signs proclaiming "Wet Paint" were taped to the railings at the entrance of the steps, and the scent of fresh toxic paint hung in the air. A few "maintenance" inmates scattered along the open stairway coating the metallic steps with institutional green paint; I cautiously stepped over each stair, hoping I would not get splatters all over my shoes.

Regardless, I still managed to pick up some of the bright color on my sneakers.

"This our room. Room #224," Sofie pointed out the 1st door on the left at the top of the stairs. Stepping through the same color mint-green doorway and noting the rather large window in the door, I was relieved we were not completely shut out-of-sight in these rooms. But I was especially surprised to see a private bathroom located immediately inside the entrance of the room.

"Are you serious?" I inquired of Sofie regarding the exclusive bathroom.

Complete with a toilet, large sink and secluded shower area, there was a large "mirror" placed above the sink. It was not glass however, as there were no mirrors or glass objects permitted anywhere within the compound. It was a large steel plate bolted to the wall that looked similar to the outside of a toaster. A very distorted view to say the least, but still the only sight I'd had of myself in months. I could barely see the gray hair on the top of my head already beginning to peek through. I knew I would have to get used to it. It was only going to get worse over the next several months.

The recently painted flat-white, 8' x 12' cement block room contained two sets of bunkbeds placed end-to-end along the wall on the right; four skinny locker-style closets, four large drawers - one for each person, and two desks, each to be shared with your *bunkie* - all placed together along the opposite wall. All of the "furniture" was constructed of metal and army brown in color. There were also four lock boxes allocated to each prisoner placed alongside the assigned bunk. A fairly sizeable window with large black bars was positioned on the opposite end of the cell to permit light into the small room. Not at all like the huge 150-bunkbed open dorms at Maryswood, I was impressed. It just kept getting better. *Surely, I must be at Prison Hilton.* I had been assigned to the top bunk again, right above Sofie. At this point, however, I had lost nearly 16 pounds, so I was no longer feeling the exertion it took to climb up onto the bunk. And I was certainly pleased to have a ladder!

"Other roomies at work right now, but you'll meet them this afternoon. I don't see your pillow. Come on, let's go get you a pillow," Sofie offered.

I followed her down the hall to the storage closet. After checking for a "softer" pillow, we grabbed one and headed back to the room. As we walked side-by-side down the hallway, I realized I was feeling fairly comfortable with Sofie, and appreciated her helpful and pleasant manner. I recalled my prayer while still on the bus to the compound: *Oh, and God? If we should have our own rooms with roommates, could I please be assigned with those who read the Bible and don't swear all the time?*

Not having met the other roommates yet, I could only dare to hope I would feel safe, and not be riddled with the constant foul language and arrogance that was so prominent at Maryswood.

We had just returned to the room when it was announced time for 10:00 am count. "Is this a standing or sitting count?" I asked.

"Sitting," she answered. "Mr. Boyd be up in about 5 minutes. CO always announce the time and give you a few minutes to get out of the bathroom, or whatever you doing to get ready. Just don't be caught in the showers when it's count time."

"How long and when can you take showers?" I inquired as I climbed up the ladder and onto my bunk, taking my place at the edge of the bed.

"Shoot, anytime just so it's not count-time, or after lights out at 11:00 every night, and no earlier than 6:00 am in the morning. Breakfast at 6:00 am to 8:00 am. Most usually have to be at work or classes by 8:00 am. Just depends on your schedule," Sofie continued. "Now shush. I hear Mr. Boyd coming up the stairs."

Answered Prayer

We both sat perfectly still while Mr. Boyd checked into all the rooms on the 2nd floor. Then we quietly laid down on our bunks as he completed his rounds on the 1st floor. "Count clear!" we finally heard him shout throughout the entire dorm.

I asked Sofie more questions, specifically how soon I would have access to use the phones. "They said we would have to wait until we were issued our card with an access code. How long does that usually take?"

"Sometimes it takes about a week. But hopefully you'll have it in the next 2-3 days," she answered.

"Oh crap! I really wanted to let my family know that I have been moved and where I am right now," I complained. "I really didn't want to have to wait a whole week."

"Look, I'll only do it this one time 'cause I ain't gettin' in trouble for this; but you can use my card for just 5 minutes to talk to your family," Sofie offered.

"Really, you would do that?" I was feeling especially good about this new roommate. Sofie was great, and I hadn't heard her say even one offensive word.

"Yeah, I'll do it this time. But you don't tell NO one I let you use it. I'm not going down for this. I'll tell them you stole it from me," she warned.

"Oh, thank you! I promise I won't say a word to anyone at all. I don't want to get into trouble either. Thank you!"

"Oh, and by the way," Sofie stated authoritatively - facing me, her clenched fists perched firmly on her ample hips, "You need to know that we have a few rules in this room. There ain't *NO* swearing or taking the Lord's name in vain, and we read the Bible every night! You got that?" she boldly asked with a stern look.

I was startled. I couldn't even breathe for a minute. *What did she just say?* "You got that?" she repeated in a firm voice.

"Uh, yeah . . . I got it," I quietly stammered out. I was at a total loss for words. God had not only heard, but very *specifically* answered my prayer. I was truly beginning to understand and believe in a God who was becoming very real to me.

"Come and hear, all of you who fear God; let me tell you what he has done for me . . . for God has surely listened and has heard my prayer." Psalm 66: 16 & 19

Sofie and I walked back down to the first floor, and she gave me a quick tour of the building. Although it was all one open area with the CO's circular desk located in the center of the atrium, she pointed out the small laundry room; the game, microwave and ironing area to the left; the small library where she worked part-time situated directly behind and to the right of the CO's desk; phone cubicles and mail pick-up boxes, as well as the medical center located near the entrance of the unit. She then directed me over to the tables set up in the game area, and quickly scrawled something down on a small torn-off piece of paper and handed it to me. "Now don't lose this and when you done, make sure you destroy that number! I can't have every conniving convict up in here using my phone card number!" she stammered out.

There was that dirty word again - convict. As much as I didn't want to have any association with a word like that, it was true. I was very much a part of this group of women who had been convicted of some kind of dreadful crime. I wasn't any different than anyone else in here. I was a sinner in every right.

"I understand. Thank you Sofie," I genuinely offered.

"You better wait until after shift change tonight to make your phone call. Mr. Boyd know you just came in, so he'll catch you on the phone," Sofie cautioned me.

"Ok, I will. Thank you." I was truly grateful for this woman who had been assigned as my bunkmate and fellow "partner in crime". I sensed the sincere desire of Sofie's heart to take me in under her wing; to guide me, protect me and teach me.

"See, I am sending an angel ahead of you to guard you along the way and to bring you to the place I have prepared."
Exodus 23:20

CHAPTER 2

❧ *Edification* ❧

n. the act or process of edifying. v. to instruct and improve especially in moral and religious knowledge. Act or process to uplift, enlighten, inform, establish, build, educate, inspire, nurture, illuminate.

"Teach me your way, LORD that I may rely on your faithfulness, give me an undivided heart, that I may fear your name." Psalm 86:11

Angel and Joy

"C'mon, get your coat. Let's go eat," Sofie instructed me. It was lunchtime, so we grabbed our coats from the hooks on back of the door and proceeded to walk over to CFS (*Central Food Service.*) It was a cold but sunny day. The warm rays from the bright sun were comforting, inviting my face to turn upward.

"Having lunchmeat and chili today," Sofie declared.

"How'd you know that?" I questioned.

"Oh, you be surprised all the secret things I know around here," as she firmly and all-knowingly winked at me.

"'Cause that's what's on the menu, silly. Menus layin' on the CO's desk, but we got one hangin' in the room too," she laughed.

"Oh, ok." I laughed and shook my head. As we walked

inside out of the wintry air and stood in line to reach the tray area, I was pleasantly surprised there were only about 50-60 inmates ahead of us in line: unlike the never-ending lines at Maryswood.

"Wow. That's crazy. No time at all to wait in these lines!" I exclaimed.

As we made our way toward the tray area, Sofie declared, "Angel and Jov both working today. But I don't see them right now. Must be working in the back." Sofie added. "They our roommates."

I knew I was hungry with no breakfast provided that morning, but the food smelled and tasted especially wonderful that particular day. The bread was fairly soft, the chili was hot, and everything tasted so much better than the unseasoned and bland dishes at the main prison. There was a large tray placed at the end of the counter, filled with fresh apples, bananas and oranges, as well as trays offering a selection of small bowls of jello, or salad with packages of dressings. And there were condiments: salt, pepper, sugar and butter, and crackers. A decent choice of beverages and juices stood in rows, not at all like the watered-down fruit-flavored powdered juice concoctions and milk at Maryswood. Yep, it was official. I was in *Prison Heaven* for sure.

Sofie and I both finished our meal, walked down the large circular 7-step concrete apron, and headed back to the dorm. "You probably get called out for work assignment sometime today or tomorrow," Sofie informed me. "Most everyone start out cleaning in the kitchen."

"That's ok. That's what I did at Maryswood for awhile," I offered. "Won't be a problem. I can clean." I was especially excited, however, to learn I would actually get paid this time - until I learned it would only be .24¢ an hour. But that was still much more than I had been receiving the previous months. My parents had originally put $20 on my books when I first arrived at Maryswood in October; and then once just before I left the main prison, my boyfriend, Don, had sent me $20. But now I could consistently have a little money on my books to order the things I needed, as well as some of the things I would like to have!

As we entered room #224 and hung our coats back up, Sofie proceeded to empty her pockets of sugar packets, and an orange. "Don't *ever* get caught taking things out of CFS," she explained, "but I need sugar for my coffee in the mornings, and I sure can't afford to buy it off commissary."

I looked at her orange. "Yea, I know, but I get hungry before bed. Supper too early for me. I don't have the money to buy snacks." And then she laughed. "Shoot. Most of the women in here steal the fruit to make *hooch,*" she went on to enlighten me.

"To make what?" I asked.

"Hooch. You know. You let the fruit ferment long enough and it eventually turns to alcohol. But you *will* automatic go to the *hole* for that if you get caught."

I knew I sure wouldn't be making *hooch*. Rancid, bitter, curdled fruit didn't even begin to sound appetizing to me in the least. I would be thrilled just to get my hands on a Coke.

I put away my belongings in my assigned drawer, locker space and lock box. I finished making my bed and made small talk with Sofie a little longer. She explained that she would be leaving soon to go downstairs to work in the library.

"Ok. I'll come down with you and check out a book so I can have something to read. But then I'm probably going to try to rest a little since I've been up since 4:00 am this morning."

"I'll be back up before afternoon count. Angel and Joy should be here by then. I'll introduce you, *Ms. Friend*," Sofie smirked.

I couldn't help but wonder if those were their real names, and if they might actually live up to them. But then again, I had to keep reminding myself we were all in prison for a reason. . . and it certainly wasn't because any of us were *angels* filled with *joy*!

Later that afternoon Sofie entered the room and woke me from a deep and restful sleep, for the 4:00 pm count. The other two ladies followed right behind her. "Come on. Get up girl. Time for count. This Angel, and this is Joy," Sofie indicated as she pointed toward each one, and then announced my name to them.

"She already know our rules, and she on board with all that," Sofie continued as she advised the two women of our earlier conversation regarding Bible-reading and appropriate language. I was still in such awe over that whole situation, but knew God had confirmed this for me as the women each nodded their head in understanding.

"Hey, that's great! What's your name again?" Angel asked me.

"Nanette," I answered.

"No. What's your last name?" she continued.

"Friend." I replied.

"Friend?" she questioned me again.

"Yes, Friend. Just like *you're my friend*," I repeated.

"Oh, no, no, no. Friend is much better. Calling you *Friend*, girlfriend!" as she giggled.

Angel was a large, approximately 5'8", overweight but fairly attractive woman with an ebony complexion in her late twenties. A bright yellow-gold stretchy band was wrapped around her head of black cornrows. She walked to her bunk with a slow, exaggerated swagger. She was a very sweet girl who really liked to talk - mostly about herself. I would soon find out she had six children: four girls and two boys, all under the age of 10. She would later tell me all of their names and ages, although I would have to ask her several times to remind me who was who.

Angel's mother was a doctor at a local hospital, and the only one available to keep Angel's children while she was in prison. This grandmother most certainly had her hands full. Oftentimes Dr. Morris was unable to bring Angel's children for visitation hours due to her very busy schedule. Angel cried about that a lot; she missed those kids terribly.

I would later learn Angel had been convicted of grand theft, extortion and check fraud. She declared she had only wanted the absolute best for her children, and had somehow obtained a beautiful large house, nice luxury van with a television and all the amenities; all the name brand shoes and clothes, Disney vacations and everything you could ever imagine for those kids.

"Girl, I wouldn't be caught dead with my kids lookin' like no street *gangstas*! Oh no, my kids don't wear nothin' but Nike, Calvin Klein, Guess, Tommy Hilfinger and North Face!" she proudly proclaimed.

Now Angel was realizing the hard truth that you actually had to go to work to provide all of those things for your family. But then, who was *I* to judge anyone at all about theft – or *any* crime for that matter? Ordered to a one-year mandatory term in the women's state prison for embezzlement and forgery of a very wealthy client, I was in no position whatsoever to even think about judging anyone else of anything at all. I needed to focus on my own crime, my own sins, and my own family.

Joy, on the other hand, was a young white girl, of whom I would later learn had two small boys, ages 4 and 6, still living at home. Her grandfather was taking care of them while she was serving out the rest of her sentence.

Long, dull, mousy light brown hair that descended clear down her back, but always worn in a ponytail or braid; her pale, blemished, and scarred complexion portrayed her inner brokenness and hardness. She went along with reading the Bible but was quick to defend herself, and you could sense she was not really believing what she read. I never did find out what she was serving time for. Joy pretty much kept to herself. I assumed it probably had something to do with drugs. Angel told me at one point that Joy had taken a bad rap for her "baby daddy."

"Her what?" I had questioned.

"You know, the father of her kids. Her *man,*" she explained.

I also learned Joy was taking classes at the on-site college, and it would be another two years before she could be released.

"Count!" Mr. Boyd yelled up the stairs. This was the 4:00 pm standing count. Positioned on the floor beside our bunk, we stood at attention as we looked straight ahead at all times, with no talking. As soon as he stepped inside the room and took note: "At ease ladies," he quietly spoke - we were then free to sit silently on our beds until count was over.

Angel and Joy had been working over at CFS in the kitchen since 4:00 am and were relieved their shifts were over. They took turns taking showers to get ready for dinner.

"What's on the menu tonight?' Sofie questioned Angel.

"It's a secret!" I giggled.

"Oh, now *you* the wise guy!" Sofie smirked.

Puzzled, Angel replied, "Fried chicken and greens."

"Oh yeah! I need me some chicken and collard greens!" Sofie exclaimed.

I was feeling exceptionally grateful and pleased to realize all of the amenities and finer features of this facility - but even more so, I was thankful for these ladies who didn't appear to fight, scream, swear, consistently trash-talk, or make me feel threatened in any way. Although the very first day, I already felt a huge sense of peace and comfort here; as well as the awareness and relief of not having to constantly look over my shoulder out of fear of retaliation or revenge.

And I will provide a place for my people Israel and will plant them so that they can have a home of their own and no longer be disturbed. Wicked people will not oppress them anymore as they did at the beginning.   1 Chronicles 17:9

Homesick

After dinner, we all walked back over to our unit. Sofie had to work a few more hours in the dorm library that evening. Joy gathered her books and also went to the library to study. That left Angel to hang out with, but that was okay. I was thankful she kept me occupied, and somewhat took my mind off of things as I anxiously awaited the later evening hours to arrive so I could call home. I felt sick to my stomach as I knew I would be calling "illegally" - and yet I was so horribly homesick and longed to hear familiar voices again.

We headed down to the game room where Angel introduced me to some of the women there. "Hey girlfriends! Wus up?" she asked as we approached two women sitting at a table playing cards. "This Tanisha and Cricket. They both good people. They all go to church and Sofie's Bible study with us," she explained.

Tanisha was a young, deeply dark-skinned girl, who was obviously very pregnant. I was surprised she was located at this facility, as all the pregnant women were most usually transported out to another lock-down facility within the state. She later explained she would soon be leaving to go back to her county jail, so she had been transferred to this location temporarily. Though shy and soft-spoken, Tanisha proudly shared she was almost seven months along now and expecting a baby boy.

Wearing her short, nappy pitch-black hair pulled up tight in a small ponytail, Tanisha's large, dark-brown square-framed, and extremely thick-lens glasses looked so out-of-place against her young and pretty face. I would later learn these were "state-issued" glasses (most likely donated used glasses) as she had not been able to obtain her own glasses yet. I understood that exact situation, as I had still not received my prescription contacts in the mail. It had been almost two months since I had asked my parents to please order my contacts to be shipped direct from the company, as I was not permitted to keep or bring in my own contacts. However, all of my mail was still in transit, trying to catch up with me, and this was now my third location.

"What's your name again? *Friend?*" That's so cool!" Wanna play cards with us?" Cricket inquired.

"Sure. That sounds great," I answered.

Cricket, an older, small but firm-statured, hard-looking white woman, sat directly to the right of me, and started up a conversation. Originally believing that Cricket was most probably in her mid-to-late 40's, her raspy, high-pitched voice caused me to believe this might be why she had acquired the nick-name of "Cricket." I would later learn she was actually only in her mid-thirties. It was very obvious the years of alcohol and drug abuse had taken a toll on her physical appearance. But she had an infectious smile and laughed a lot. I admired her attitude. She just didn't seem to let anything bother her that much. At least not on the outside.

We played cards for a short while and Tanisha offered popcorn she had made. It smelled so good, and the aroma brought back fond memories of when I would make buttered popcorn for my own kids; but I was feeling too nervous to eat anything.

Becoming more anxious as I continued to watch the clock and anticipated the best time to call home, I realized Mr. Boyd had finally finished his shift for the evening. Regardless, I still needed to wait until I knew that both Jennifer and Don would be home.

My youngest daughter, Jennifer, only 16 years-old at this time, was my last child still living at home; and Don, my boyfriend of almost four years, lived with us in our tiny apartment. Things had not gone well at all when I first learned I would have to serve a mandatory one-year prison sentence for embezzlement from one of my clients. (In a very poor, but drastic attempt to keep my small start-up business afloat, I told myself I was only "borrowing" the nearly $170,000. Regardless, near the end, I couldn't stay afloat with all the payroll, insurance, utilities, office equipment and furniture, rent, taxes, upkeep, etc.) Originally told I would not serve any prison time as this was my very first (and only) offense, now my family were all scrambling to readjust and work together since my sentencing and imprisonment . . . and I eagerly awaited to speak with each of them again.

Angel and I finished playing cards, said our goodbyes to Tanisha and Cricket, and headed back upstairs. Angel was especially tired and wanted to get ready for bed. However, not without filling me in about her precious six children. But I genuinely understood. She was so homesick after only serving half of her 4-year sentence. I couldn't imagine. I didn't know how I was going to get through yet another ten months in prison.

Angel cried as she explained her oldest daughter was about to turn 11, and that her mother was the one who had to explain to Aylissa about becoming a young woman.

"I'm just sick about all that. I should have been there to talk to my own daughter about getting her first cycle. But I learned my lesson. I just pray to God I can go home sometime soon," she explained as tears ran down her face. "I keep applying for early judicial release, but the judge denies it and won't let me go home."

"What's that?" I asked.

"Judicial release? It's when you ask the judge to let you get out early," she explained.

I was curious and wanted to know more about this early release program - but I also knew it was getting late and I wanted to call home. I couldn't let Angel know I would be using Sofie's phone card, so I explained I had to go down and talk to Sofie for a minute. I lightly hugged her large body and told her I would be back.

"I'll see you later. Get some sleep," I whispered as I left the room. I could hear her softly crying, and knew she would soon drift off to sleep.

"He heals the brokenhearted and binds up their wounds."
Psalm 147:3

Betrayed

It was now about 8:00 pm as I leapt down the steps and headed to the library desk where I told Sofie I was going to call home now. "Okay but watch your back. And only take a few minutes," she instructed.

"I will. Thank you," I quietly muttered as I proceeded to the semi-private phone banks located about twenty feet from the CO's desk. I knew I would have to speak quietly.

My heart was pounding in anticipation as I waited for someone to pick up on the other end. Yet, I was especially nervous as I punched in Sofie's phone code. Would one of the staff in the prison be listening in to my phone call? I would have to be very selective with my words. How was I going to say I just got here when Sofie had already been here for almost a year now? *Oh, please God. Please do not let anyone hear my words tonight.*

I heard Don's deep voice say "hello?"- and then the automated voice of the operator requesting permission to accept a collect call from a prisoner housed at the Women's State Reform Center.

"Yes," he quietly responded. "Hello?"

I swallowed hard and my heart raced even faster. "Hey. I'm so glad you're home. I wanted to let you know that I've been moved to the Pre-Release Center now," I blurted out. So much for selective wording.

"Where?" He answered.

"To the Pre-Release Center on Wirth Road in the South Dover area. I'm only about 45 minutes from home now. I really hope you can come and see me soon. I miss you so much, I can't stand it." Tears welled up in my eyes and a lump choked my throat.

"How soon will I be able to come?" Don asked.

"I don't know. I do know I have to fill out a lot of paperwork stating who I want to visit me. You have to be specified on the visitation list to come in. I will have to get your driver's license number, date of birth, social security number, etc. They'll run everything to make sure you're not a convicted felon before you're allowed to come in. But I'll get all that later. I can't talk very long. I just wanted to let you know where I am now. I love you and miss you so much," I tried to keep from crying.

"I love and miss you too. I'm really not doing very well. I'm trying to hold it together, but things are just really hard right now," Don explained.

"What do you mean? Are you okay? Is Jennifer okay?"

"We'll talk about it later. I really want to come and see

you. Here, let me have you talk to Jen now." He passed the phone to my daughter.

I could hear Jennifer softly ask Don, "Are you okay?" I knew he was upset that I was not home with them. I knew he was probably crying, and it was breaking my heart - all the pain I had caused him and everyone in my family.

"Hi Mom. How are you doing?" my cherished daughter asked.

Through muffled tears I cried "I'm good, honey. I really am. I've been moved closer to home and it's *so* much better here. And now I can have visitors. I have to fill out a lot of paperwork to allow you to come in, but I can't wait to see you and everyone. I miss you so much. I'm so sorry for everything. I love you. I really do."

"I know you do Mom. I love you too. Everything is going to be okay. I promise." Bless her heart. She was repeating back to me the very same words I would always say to my children when they were little, when things had been so hard and difficult for us.

Only a junior in high school this year, I could see that she was maturing in a way I had not recognized before. The youngest of four, Jen had pretty much been spoiled a little more than the others. A single mother to my children from the time she had been a baby, my kids had all faced many challenges in their early lives. But this was by far the worst thing that had ever happened to us.

"I don't even know where to begin. But someday I will try to explain everything to you Jen. I am so sorry," I said through tears. "And I'm really sorry honey, but I have to get off the phone now."

"Okay. I understand. Oh, Mom? There was some lady

who called here from the jail who said her name was Nora and that you told her she was allowed to charge her phone calls to your number, but I refused the call. For some reason that didn't sound right to me. Should I have done that?" she asked.

Immediately I recalled the older, grandmotherly black woman at Maryswood who had counseled and shared so many wonderful things with me from the Bible. The day before I left the maximum facility, she had asked me for my phone number. I recalled being somewhat surprised at her request, knowing that we would not be able to be in contact for over a year (You are not permitted to have any contact with another inmate, or someone with a felony conviction once you leave the prison). Now I was shocked, and immediately infuriated. I had trusted this woman whom I had believed to be my friend, as well as a godly woman. How could she use her presumed love of God to betray me?

"Bitterly she weeps at night, tears are on her cheeks. Among all her lovers there is no one to comfort her. All her friends have betrayed her; they have become her enemies.

Lamentations 1:2

And yet a valuable lesson – just as so many people had trusted *me,* I had lied to, and betrayed them as well. God was righteously teaching me in a way that I painfully needed to experience for myself. Not at all that God had ever desired for me to go to prison . . . I managed to do that all of my own accord. Nor that God would ever want me to be in pain or to suffer needlessly. But in His infinite wisdom, He understood that how could I truly experience and learn of the immeasurable pain and suffering I had inflicted upon so many others, if He did not allow me *to be instructed and improved, especially in moral and spiritual knowledge?* God's only desire for me was to be *enlightened, informed, educated, inspired and nurtured (Edification)* of who He was, and of the woman He created me to be. At that very moment, I also realized I had just lied to and gone against the rules and regulations that were expected of me: I had indeed "plotted" and "schemed" to use the phone that very night. I was ashamed.

"No, honey. You did right. Do not allow her or anyone else at all to charge anything to our phone bill. Thank you. I love you. Good night. I'll call again soon."

I hung up the phone and darted straight to the stairwell. Head held down, I climbed the steps and tried so hard to ensure it was not obvious that I was crying or upset in any way. With a huge lump in my throat, I entered the room and was thankful that Angel was already asleep, and that Joy and Sofie were still downstairs. I just needed some quiet time right then.

I washed up, brushed my teeth, got ready for bed and crawled into my "safe place" with God. I pulled the covers up and rested my head on an actual pillow with a pillowcase for the first time in months.

In that moment, I felt as though I could have possibly understood what Corrie Ten Boom *("The Hiding Place"- TooBosss Publishers,1971)* experienced as she described the soft, white and clean bed she would eventually sleep in after months spent in a Nazi concentration camp – and that she had finally felt *safe*. I *knew* this could not even begin to compare to the horrific conditions she had experienced of sleeping upon a dirty, insect-infested bed of hay. And my "new" bunk could most definitely not be compared to that of a "soft, white bed" – but at that moment, I was so grateful for my own space: a clean, quiet and "safe" space - with a ladder and a pillow.

I was still exhausted from the previous day of little sleep. I turned over and faced the wall. I didn't know how long it would be before the other ladies would be upstairs - I only knew I wanted to talk to God, and then go to sleep. I held my well-worn paperback bible in my hands as if it were an irreplaceable precious gift - of which it truly was.

How peaceful it was in this room – unlike the huge, open, brilliantly lit and noisy dorms of Maryswood. I closed my eyes.

. . .

"God, thank you for everything you have given to me today. Thank you for bringing me to this safe place. I know there are still so many things I do not understand and need to learn, but I know you are teaching me, and watching over me. I have not been a good person or an example to my children. What was wrong with me? What was I even thinking? Please help me God. Please show me what you want me to do." . . . I continued to pray . . . and then softly cried myself to sleep.

"Hezekiah turned his face to the wall and prayed to the LORD, . . . the word of the LORD came to him: "Go back and tell Hezekiah, the ruler of my people, 'This is what the LORD, the God of your father David, says: I have heard your prayer and seen your tears; I will heal you."   2 Kings 20:2, 4-5

CHAPTER 3

❧ *Communication* ❧

n. The impartation or interchange of thoughts, opinions, or information by verbal speech, writings or signs, symbols or behavior. Something interchanged or transmitted, expressing ideas effectively; body language, eye contact, personal rapport.

"Show me your ways, LORD, teach me your paths".
Psalm 25:4

Nothing but Time

I never did hear Sofie or Joy come back into the room that night. I was quickly awakened and startled however, when I realized the brilliant gleam of a flashlight glaring directly into my eyes as the night-shift CO made her rounds for the 4:00 am count.

"Friend?" she questioned me.

"Yes," I drowsily answered.

"Ok. Just checking. Your first night here," she whispered, more of a fact rather than a question.

"Yes ma'am."

She quickly checked the other women and abruptly left the room. I could barely hear her moving up and down the hallway as she stepped into each room. I heard a few of the toilets flushing as the interruption of an otherwise peaceful night had been disturbed.

I laid awake a little while longer as I readjusted to my new and *quiet* surroundings. The shadows of the bright lights from the hallway made for a perfect soft night light into our room. This was nothing at all like the intense "stadium" overhead lights, or the never-ending noise prevalent in the large open dorms at Maryswood. It was then I realized I had forgotten to ask anyone what time we were required to be up for inspection, as well as morning cleaning and chores. No one else even stirred, however. So, I turned back over and slept for another two or possibly three hours.

Eventually, I heard Joy and Angel getting up and off to work. When I heard Sofie stirring from the lower bunk beneath me, I opened my eyes slightly and asked,

"What time is it? What time do we have to be up and ready?"

"It's about 5:45 am. You gotta be up, dressed and have the room cleaned by 8 am. Breakfast at 6 am to 8 am. You don't have to go over if you don't want to, but they got some good donuts today," Sofie offered.

"That's it? There's no inspection?" I surprisingly asked. Other than the weekends, there were always 5:00 am cleaning and inspections at Maryswood.

"No. CO come and check throughout the day. Room just better be clean, beds made and no playin' going on," she warned. "Most jobs or classes, you gotta be there by 8 am. I don't have to be downstairs until 10 am on days I work, but I don't gotta work today. You wanna go get some donuts with me?" she asked again.

"They got donuts here? Nah, I'm not really a breakfast person," I vaguely sighed. "And it's too cold out there."

"Suit yourself. But you missing out on some good breakfast today."

"I'll get up pretty soon. I'm going to take a shower," I explained as I rolled back over and tucked my head under the covers for an extra thirty minutes of restful peace.

"Ok, but don't be playin'. I'll be back and show you where the cleaning things are. It'll take us 'bout twenty minutes to clean this place," she instructed.

Eventually, I crawled down the ladder, gathered my things together and prepared to take a shower to awaken my drowsy demeanor. As I stepped into the warm and steamy shower and pulled the curtain securely, I breathed a deep sigh of heartfelt relief to finally feel peaceful and untroubled in this new place. With no longer the restriction of a 3-minute time limit for a shower as permitted at Maryswood, I allowed the warm, balmy water to slowly pour down my face, my long dark hair, and my back. It felt so wonderfully comforting upon my skin, and I could sense the tension and anxiety lifting from my being. *Thank you, God,* I sighed.

As I finished washing up, I made a mental list of a few of the very first things I would want to buy from commissary: razors, tweezers, nail files (cardboard only), Q-tips and personal products to feel clean and refreshed again; as well as soda pop and chips, of course. I wasn't sure how long it would be before what little money I still had left on my books at Maryswood would be transferred to this center, nor when I would begin to start receiving additional money, either from home or from my job here. But I had waited this long, so a little while longer wouldn't make much difference.

I had grown accustomed to waiting on everything by now: letters from home, money, contacts for my eyes, the ability to make phone calls, work assignments, and for another day to go by that I could mark off my calendar. With nothing but time on my hands, however, it had become increasingly more difficult each day as I would constantly think and worry about what was going on in the outside world: my children, my bills, my boyfriend, my job (or lack of), and any number of other responsibilities. I was finding it hard to cope with the fact that I no longer had any control of, nor could take care of all the things I needed to do in my life. My biggest worry of all, of course, was leaving my youngest daughter at home. How could I help her, protect her, be the one stable force she had ever known, when I was locked away from her young life? My heart ached with the pain of my guilt, my sin, and the inability to do anything at all. I felt so hopeless.

Time had indeed become my enemy. And yet, it wouldn't be until much later during my prison time I would eventually realize that although God did expect for me to be held responsible for my very poor decisions; He would utilize this valuable time to take me out of my time and comfort zone so He could capture my 100% attention. Otherwise, how could He ever teach me, mold me, communicate to me, or let me know that He loved me . . . if I had remained in the outside world - where I would *never* focus on Him? This was *His* time for me. I needed the discipline, the understanding, the knowledge, the wisdom, the love and the forgiveness that only God could provide. And eventually, I needed to heal from all the self-condemnation, brokenness and hatred I had allowed to permeate my heart and soul.

There is a time for everything, and a season for every activity under the heavens:

A time to be born and a time to die, a time to plant and a time to uproot,

A time to kill and a time to heal, a time to tear down and a time to build,

A time to weep and a time to laugh, a time to mourn and a time to dance,

A time to scatter stones and a time to gather them, a time to embrace and a time to refrain from embracing,

A time to search and a time to give up, a time to keep and a time to throw away,

A time to tear and a time to mend, a time to be silent and a time to speak,

A time to love and a time to hate, a time for war and a time for peace. . .

Whatever is has already been, and what will be has been before; and God will call the past to account.

Ecclesiastes 3:1-8;15

The Good News

But the angel said to them, "Do not be afraid. I bring you Good News that will cause great joy for all the people."

Luke 2:10

About the time I was dressed and combing through my wet and tangled hair; Sofie arrived back at the room grinning from ear to ear. She pulled out 2 hard-boiled eggs and 2 sugar-coated donuts wrapped up in napkins from her pockets. "Girl, you gotta eat somethin'," she insisted.

"You're gonna get busted one of these days," as I shook my head in complete disbelief.

"Here, I got salt for the eggs too. You'll have to get some juice downstairs if you want," she went on.

"I appreciate it, I really do. But don't be stealing food for me. I don't want you to get caught!"

"Aaww. I do it all the time," Sofie offered.

"And you're not worried about getting into trouble?"

"Yeah, but I haven't yet and I'm good at it," she laughed.

"Girl, you're not right! You're a bad influence on me!" I softly laughed, as I took a few bites from one of the sugary donuts. Eventually I would understand the only reason we very seldom had donuts, was because they were ready to be thrown out before expiration date at the grocery stores. No matter - they tasted exceptionally good at that moment! I closed my eyes and breathed another sigh of contentment. *Mmm good! Thank you for small miracles Lord!* I thought to myself. Sofie interrupted my bliss. "Come on. Hurry up. We gotta get this room cleaned. When we done cleanin', we'll check for mail and stop at the CO's desk to see if you got a job assignment yet," she instructed.

We quickly headed down to the cleaning closet and gathered up a broom, bucket, mop, sponges, cleaning supplies and dusting rags. After sweeping and mopping the floors, dusting the room, washing down the sink, toilet, and shower, we carried the supplies back downstairs and placed in the appropriate walk-in closet.

We then made our way over to the large wall located to the left of the CO's desk and checked the bulletin board for menus, notices regarding upcoming meetings, sign-up sheets for additional programs, and other designated news and important information. To the right of the notifications, Sofie reached into the open mail slot designated for room #224 for any possible mail.

"Nah, only Angel got mail today. We all have the same box for our room, but don't ever take nobody else's mail! I never really get anything. Sometimes from my sister, or my mom, or my son, Clarence. I keep hoping I might get some money from Mom sometimes. But she don't really have any money either."

"Friend?" Mr. Boyd looked my way as we approached the CO's desk.

"Yes sir," I hesitantly responded. *How did he know my name?* I thought to myself. *Either he has a really good memory, or I was in deep trouble for using Sofie's phone card!*

"You need to report to the medical unit for a physical and bloodwork at 11:15 am. Don't be late."

Relieved, I answered "Yes sir. Can you please tell me if I will be getting a work assignment anytime soon?"

"Oh, so you *want* to work?" he half-grinned. "I'm sure we can find something for you to do around here! No, I haven't received any orders for you yet. But I'll let you know if I get anything over here today," he continued.

"Ok, thank you, Mr. Boyd," I answered.

As we turned to walk away, I pulled on Sofie's shirt sleeve and whispered in her ear "You know that's my next husband, don't you?" I giggled as we ran up the stairs.

"Girl, you crazy! And don't even be sayin' that stuff 'round here! These women up in here turn you in for saying stuff like that about staff. Anything to get you in trouble. Besides, he's married to another CO in here."

"Oh, come on, I was just kidding," I instantly reacted.

"Don't matter. They take you down for anything they can get on you. These women be shady for real. Don't be playin'. You in prison girl!" Sofie scolded me in her best "motherly" fashion.

I knew she was only trying to protect me. And I knew she was right as I recalled my disconcerting experience with Nora attempting to charge all her phone calls to my home phone number. I had really believed I could trust her, but she only used that trust to try and scam me. *Humm. . .* another lesson well learned . . . it's all different when someone else is lying to and stealing from *you.*

"Ok I hear you. I really do. I promise. I'm not even tryin' to get in any more trouble than I am right now. I just wanna do my time and go home."

"Good. Now help me write up some "Scripture notes" for my bible study tonight," as she searched for paper, pens and scissors from our shared desk drawer.

"You allowed to have scissors?" I was astounded as she pulled out a very small, child-size, pink handled and round-tip pair of scissors.

"No, not supposed to really. I took them from the library," as she matter-of-factly grabbed her bible and a small devotional booklet from her locker. *Why was I not surprised?* I had to snicker to myself.

"Get your bible too," she ordered.

Obediently, I picked up my 4"x 6", red paperback copy of the **Good News** bible, a graduation gift from my aunt and uncle many years prior. I had never opened its pages until I had arrived at Maryswood in October. Until that point – and then only after several weeks with no access of anything at all to read - I had never even read the bible . . . ever.

Raised a strict and faithful Catholic all my life (and *before* Vatican II in 1963, which eventually changed a lot of the rituals and ways we learned about Jesus - i.e., now speaking in English rather than Latin), I had been taught that only the priests were permitted to read and interpret the words of the bible to the congregation.

The large family bible situated prominently and carefully on the built-in bookshelf of my childhood home, high above the reach of my little-girl arms, held copies of birth, death, baptism and other sacramental certificates and decrees. This bible was never intended to be something we would ever read: simply a highly revered and impressive soft, red leather-bound book with gold gilt-edged pages, and the words "Holy Bible" notably written in sizeable gold letters on the front cover – carefully displayed upon the shelf.

By this point, however, I was slowly beginning to learn and understand a lot more of the many stories of this "Jesus" my great-grandmother had told me about when I was a little girl. Memories of watching Billy Graham on "Mammy's" little black and white television, I would begin to learn there was something more to Christmas day than presents and large family gatherings; or that Easter was a fun, egg-hunting event. I understood these were sacred holidays regarding His birth and death - although I truly had no understanding of the significance regarding His resurrection and eventually our salvation.

This gift of the ***Good News*** bible that I was now reading, however, only contained the *New Testament* – the life and ministry of Jesus. (It would not be until later while in prison, that I would understand there was an *"Old Testament"* of the bible, as well!) While I had begun to read my paperback bible while still at Maryswood, I was still often confused. Most of the time it was very difficult for me to understand the value or the meaning behind the stories Matthew, Mark, Luke and John (disciples) were describing. And I certainly didn't understand why they were all telling the same story over and over again. . . and who were these "prophets" they kept referring to (Old Testament)? I had so much to learn.

What I was absorbing so far was that Jesus, who was born of a young virgin woman, gathered and taught his followers of whom he instructed to spread the "Good News" . . . that we were all sinners; but that He loved us so much, He willingly faced horrific torture, suffering and eventual death on the cross for our sins to be forgiven - and to be taken away forever.

Thank you for your sacrifice dear Lord . . . because I certainly didn't feel that I had deserved or could ever be forgiven for the sins I had committed against my victim, my children, or my family. What I would eventually have to ask myself, however; was I understanding this as religious teachings and beliefs, or *true faith*? I *still* had so much to learn.

Red Letters

We scrambled back downstairs to the tables in the library to carefully and thoughtfully select short one or two sentence scripture readings. Sofie had also somehow obtained several sheets of white paper – *I was afraid to ask.* She began to cut the sheets into several small strips of paper, approximately 2"x 4" in size.

"Ok, now write down some verses on the paper and put them in this jar," as she shoved a tall, empty, round plastic coffee container toward me. "Then tonight, everyone will pull one out and read it out loud. They need to look it up and say what it's 'bout," Sofie explained as she continued to cut up the strips of paper.

"Go ahead and pick out some readings," she instructed.

I really wasn't sure what I was looking for. "What do you want me to pick out?"

After a thoughtful sigh, "Uhm. Ok, look up verses that Jesus said 'bout encouragement or hope. And that He loves us no matter what. You know, the ones in red letters," she explained.

"Oh, I know what those are!" While still at Maryswood, I had learned during a bible study, that the words specifically spoken by Jesus were highlighted in red letters. I was fascinated that I was actually able to read for myself the very words, instruction and promises that Jesus wanted us to acquire from Him.

I scoured the pages of my paperback bible, searching through the 1st book of Matthew when I came upon the very first words Jesus spoke to His disciples:

"Follow me, and I will make you fishers of men."

Matthew 4:19

From there I proceeded to search with anticipation of what other words of great wisdom, teachings and hope Jesus provided to His followers. I had previously read through these chapters as nothing more than stories *about* Jesus. Now I realized He was actually speaking these words *to me*.

To me, a sinner, a liar, a thief.

How could He possibly love me or forgive me?

And yet, here were His very real *red letter* words telling

me that He did love me, and forgive me, and wanted nothing but the very best for me.

"Ask and it will be given to you; seek and you will find; knock and the door will be opened to you."   Matthew 7:7

"Which of you, if your son asks for bread, will give him a stone? Or if he asks for a fish, will give him a snake? If you, then, though you are evil, know how to give good gifts to your children, how much more will your Father in heaven give good gifts to those who ask him!"   Matthew 7:9-11

As I continued to read through the verses, I was becoming more captivated by the teachings, inspiration and words of this man, Jesus. I was understanding more and more that He was indeed, communicating directly to *me* His words, promises, love and hope written throughout the books of his disciples.

Needles, Nudity and Nonsense

It was approaching 11:00 am and almost time for me to report to the medical facility for my physical and bloodwork.

"I gotta go in a minute Sophie," I reminded her.

"I know. See you later. Catch up with you at lunch."

I finished penning the last verse I had selected and shoved the dozen or so scripture readings I had written out into the plastic coffee jar. "See you later," I repeated back to her, and then made my way to the medical area located near the entrance of our unit, where I announced my presence.

"Have a seat. Someone be right with you," I was

instructed by one of the inmates working in the reception area.

I sat just outside the door and watched as some of the other inmates strolled in and out of the building. Each time the door was opened, I could feel the cold air whisk by me with fresh icy wind, as it almost took my breath away.

"Friend? Come on back." I was directed by the nurse into one of the rooms. Further instructed to allow her to search my arms for a good vein in order to draw blood, I turned my head away and took a deep breath as I tried to remain calm and composed. I really was a big baby when it came to needles. I always hoped if anyone ever tried to kill me, they would shoot me with one well-aimed bullet; but *please* do not stab me with a knife, needles, fishhooks or anything else that would slowly and excruciatingly penetrate my skin and make me die a slow and painful death!

"Oh you are so dramatic!" my Mom used to tell me when I was young. Maybe - but I was serious.

"Ok, you're good," as she withdrew the needle and placed a bandage over my *wound*. "Everything off and put on this gown. I'll be back in a few minutes," the nurse continued.

Well at least I had a gown to put on! That was encouraging. Eventually the nurse announced her presence and proceeded with enquiries of medical history, current medications, allergies, and a plethora of other necessary need-to-know questions. She promised to try to track down my contacts for me, which I greatly appreciated.

"Doctor will be in in a few minutes," she added as she gathered her paperwork and headed out of the exam room.

As I sat at the end of the examination table, I looked

around at the bare white cement block walls surrounding me. There was a small wooden table situated in the corner containing some clipboards, medical forms and books. A metal tray with wheels was located near the end of the table held a white towel and equipment for checking vitals, ears, throat and other body parts.

Eventually, "Hello," a rather short, dark and fairly overweight foreign man stepped inside the room. He had a full, bushy black mustache, beard and eyebrows. I wasn't quite sure what nationality he might be, although his thick accent indicated possibly Middle East, India or other distant and unfamiliar country to me. He introduced himself, but I couldn't recall his remote and unusual name.

What I did recall, however, was a very unpleasant, awkward, and embarrassing "medical" exam. Although I had fully expected the nurse to return to the room with him, the doctor closed the door and initially began by asking several questions and making pleasant small talk with me. Upon checking my ears, eyes, and throat; listening to my heart and taking my pulse, he was quick to change his demeanor. The doctor proceeded to very deliberately instruct me to lay back on the table and place my feet in the cold metal stirrups attached to the end of the table. I was shaken as he continued to fully examine me without a female attendant in the room. I was now growing very uncomfortable and offended by this man. The nurse did eventually step back in the room, but not before I had been stripped of my gown and my dignity.

"How old are you?" he inquisitively asked as he glanced through my paperwork.

"44," I obediently responded.

In his thick accent, "Your body in very good shape for your age. Very good," as I watched his eyebrows rise in approval, and his eyes and hands continue with the undignified exam. I felt so ashamed and humiliated. I looked to the nurse standing at the small prep table, hoping to catch a surprised look from her, or for her intervention of the doctor's inappropriate words and actions.

But she never looked up. I thought it might be possible that she could interpret his wording as a professional approval of keeping my physical health intact; but to me it was the demeanor and unacceptable way he looked and touched me in every aspect.

This was not the routine or mannerism of a professional medical doctor. This was absolute appalling and unnecessary nonsense and exploitation in every way. All I could think was, this was just one more example of the many demeaning ways I had felt exploited within the system. And yet, the true horror of it was that as bad as it was, I really did not have a say about anything regarding staff, rules or regulations. As a convicted thief, liar and embezzler, I had no rights in this place, and things could possibly go very wrong for me. If it was ever perceived that in any given situation of possible "retaliation," *I* could be the one to suffer the consequences.

I was certain there were many of the women who did make false statements and accusations against staff. Now I truly understood what Sofie was trying to tell me – that you can never say anything about or against the prison staff. All I could do was lie on that table in deep humiliation and shame. Other than an actual physical or sexual abuse claim, how could I ever prove anything he ever said or did to me was inappropriate?

"Ok, you can get dressed now," the nurse instructed as the doctor left the room. I quickly pulled my arms and legs through my undergarments and "state scrubs" and attempted to regain my composure. I was furious, hurt and degraded. I was shaking and my heart was beating rapidly.

Why, God? Why? I don't understand! I know I am a horrible person, but why do these things keep happening to me? And I had felt so safe in this new place! was all I could think as I held back the tears.

I ran up the stairs to my room, and quickly climbed the ladder to my bunk. Sofie had just come back up from the library to get ready to go to lunch. "Whoa! What's going on with you?" she inquired of my despondent and hopeless disposition.

"It's not fair Sofie! What's up with that quack of a doctor they have here?" I cried out to her, shaking with infuriation and rage.

"Oh, I see you have met the foot doctor!" she answered.

"What? The foot doctor? What do you mean?" I questioned.

"Yea, they all bring that crazy fool all the way up here from Clintonburg twice a week 'cause they can't get nobody else! He ain't nothin' but an inept foot doctor and a pervert! Why what happened?" she persisted.

"You mean everyone knows about this quack?" I surprisingly asked. "I thought it was the law that there has to be a female nurse or attendant in the room with you when a doctor performs a complete examination? He was a total jerk and made me feel so nasty!" as the tears rolled down my cheeks. "There's no sense in it! Isn't there anything I can say or do to report him?" I lashed out in total disbelief.

"Oh, you can report him for sure. But it won't do you no good. You forget where you are girlfriend. They all think you just trying to cause trouble or something. You don't want to be dragged through the mud and have that all go on your record for being a troublemaker. You just gotta let it go girl, and that's the sad truth!" she explained. "Come on, let's go to lunch. I'll stay with you," Sofie attempted to console me.

I sure didn't feel like any lunch right then. This was yet another huge awakening for me. I had sadly and unwillingly experienced many other situations of mental, physical and sexual abuse throughout my life - and most of the time from people I thought I could trust and love. But I guess I still held out hope that out in the "real" world, the rules and laws would have to apply to people to be honest, professional and trustworthy in their profession.

Wow. Indeed, another realization for me. For here am I: a liar, a thief and a convicted felon of the law for hurting and deceiving those who had trusted *me*. I knew it was an acutely disturbing truth for me to face, and yet deep down, I knew that God was teaching and counseling me out of His deepest love for me - as a true Father should.

Keep me from deceitful ways; be gracious to me and teach me your law.   *Psalm 119:29*

CHAPTER 4

❧ Salvation ❧

adj. Deliverance from the power and effects of sin; the agent or means that effects liberation from ignorance or illusion; preservation from destruction or failure; deliverance from danger or difficulty; rescue.

How shall we escape if we ignore so great a salvation? This salvation, which was first announced by the Lord, was confirmed to us by those who heard him.　　　*Hebrews 2:3*

Maybe . . .

Still reeling in a downward spiral from my disconcerting incident with the prison "foot" doctor, I trudged along the footpath alongside Sofie back to our dorm. I abhorred the fact that once again, I would find myself falling prey to the lies, deceit, and corruption of evil men of this world. *Why God? Why the physical, mental and sexual abuse of those I should have trusted to love me, protect me and take care of me? Why did I constantly feel I wasn't good enough, pretty enough, smart enough, skinny enough? Maybe if I had been a better person, worked harder, been stronger or more beautiful, maybe . . . maybe.*

I could only assume I had done something to deserve this. Self-blame and condemnation had always been my only recourse when I got hurt. I knew I would have to change. I would have to do better. I would have to ask God to make *me* be a better person.

And yet, deep-down, I also knew that I blamed God for not protecting me, providing for me, or loving me the way I thought He should. I had always believed in God and His goodness, as my great-grandmother (Mammy) had taught me, but I had eventually come to the conclusion that His love and care just weren't meant for me. If only I had been a better Christian. . . *maybe.*

"Friend?" Mr. Boyd motioned for me to approach his desk as Sofie and I entered the dorm immediately after lunch.

"Yes sir?" I answered as I proceeded to the circular station.

Leaning back in his swivel chair, he adjusted his reading glasses perched at the end of his nose and announced:

"You have work assignment tonight at CFS *(Central Food Service)*. Report to Miss *C* in the kitchen promptly after 4:00 pm count. She'll get you set up."

Then he added "Make sure you stop back here at the desk to sign out before you leave."

"Yes, sir. Thank you!" My mood immediately changed from self-pity and self-criticism to that of hope and encouragement once again. I was excited to have this opportunity to work, to help pass the time as quickly as possible; but more importantly to have some form of structure and control of my life again. I needed self-esteem. I hated having to depend on others to help me. I didn't want that anymore. I would work hard and be strong and get through this all on my own, just like I always had.

"Yeees! I can finally start working again!" I told Sofie enthusiastically as we headed toward the stairs.

"Whoa! Don't get too excited there, girlfriend. You know they call it work for a reason," she half-heartedly laughed.

"I know, but I don't care. I need money and I need to be doing something. It's been almost two months and I'm going crazy with nothing to do to make this time go by. By the way, how do I sign up for the extra programs and classes?" I inquired.

"Go on back over there and look through the bulletin board for available classes, and then ask Mr. Boyd for sign-up sheets. Not everything goin' be available to you right away. You may have to wait 'til the next class starts, or see if you even qualify for some programs," Sofie instructed.

"Ok, thanks. I'll be up later," I cheerfully responded as I briskly walked over to the bulletin board and looked through several flyers, notices, and options posted that I might be interested in or qualify for. There was a multitude of information regarding college classes beginning with the winter quarter that would resume after the first of the year; however, this was only the first week of December. GOALS program (8-week class setting attainable goals for your life), Theft class (for those who had committed crimes of theft, larceny, embezzlement or robbery), Bible studies, computer skills, financial planning and exercise classes were among some of the programs I was interested in. I stopped at the CO's desk and asked Mr. Boyd for sign-up sheets, as well as the paperwork required to fill out for qualifying visitor's list, work skills, qualifications, and other pertinent information related to being placed in appropriate classes. *This should keep me busy for a while.*

"Thank you, Mr. Boyd," as I bounced back up the stairs and to my room. Sofie was already lying in the bed reading through her bible in preparation for the bible study that night.

"So did you find anything you wanted?" she raised up her head to see my response.

"Yeah, I think there are a couple of things. Looks like most of them I will have to wait for a while to start."

"Told ya. But you'll be busy 'nough once you start workin' all the time," she offered as she rolled back over on her side.

"I know. Just wanted to check out dates and options. Oh, you do know I won't be able to go to bible study tonight? I have to be at CFS after count," I offered as an afterthought.

"Yeah, I heard Mr. Boyd. You'll be ok. You got the teacher as your bunkie!" she chuckled.

I scrambled up the ladder to my bunk to look through the paperwork that had been provided to me, and eagerly began to fill out the various forms and information sheets. Shortly thereafter and feeling that I had completed as much information as possible for the moment, I turned over and rested for a short while before 4:00 pm count. As I closed my eyes, I was already feeling much better, and beginning to sense that I was somewhat back in charge of my life. As per my usual mind set, I had convinced myself once again that if I could only take back the control in my life, I would prove that I was resilient and able to do this all on my own. I didn't need anyone else. Not anymore.

"They claim to know God, but by their actions they deny him."
Titus 1:16

Miss "C"

"What do you prefer? Shall I come to you with a rod of discipline, or shall I come in love and with a gentle spirit?"
1 Corinthians 4:21

The loud sound of Angel's booming laugh upon entrance into our room awoke me from a very short, yet restful nap. "Oh, sorry Friend!" she exclaimed as she continued to carry on about an event that occurred in the kitchen that day.

"That girl be crazy for real! Stealing those knives and then sayin' she gonna sharpen them like she not in prison or somethin'! Don't *nobody* **touch** those knives without Miss C tellin' 'em it ok! That girl done lost her mind!" as she continued to laugh at the audacity of someone thinking they could just go into the kitchen office and confiscate the knives from the metal closet. "Then she have the nerve to say she just wanted to sharpen them! Oh, Miss C took her down good! Called out the guards and everything! She wasn't playin'! 'Ol girl gonna be up in that hole for a while now! That just made my day for real!" Angel snorted.

"Girl, you crazy! I suppose you over there laughing the whole time it was going down!" Sofie commented, shaking her head.

"You know it girlfriend!" Angel chuckled. "It was a hoot! Ol' girl must have got her hands on something up in here. Don't nobody do something so crazy."

I immediately thought about the *hooch* (alcohol derived from fermented fruit) that Sofie had told me about. I sure didn't know how or what these women might be able to get their "hands on" otherwise.

"See what you got to look forward to?" Sofie asked me. "Bunch of crazy people up in here!" But I had already pretty much assumed that of *all* of us, to end up in a place like this anyhow. However, recalling my innate fear of knives, I was not amused.

"Yeah . . . great," I answered her with a half-smile.

"Friend goin' to work over at CFS with y'all now," Sofie informed Joy and Angel, adding that I had been assigned to the kitchen and would report to Miss C after count.

"Hey! We'll be workin' with you if you work the day shift, and I'll help you if you need anything," Angel offered.

"Ok, thanks. I'm sure I'm going to need it," I replied.

"Count!" Mr. Boyd brashly hollered up the stairs. We immediately scampered to take our standing position at the side of our bunks. Angel was still giggling out loud to herself.

"Girl! Don't be holdin' us up! Now shush up for real!" Sofie scolded.

Joy, who had not been amused at all, nor able to get a word in edgewise, could only roll her eyes and shake her head in disbelief. She really wasn't one to make light of most things, being a no-nonsense kind of woman.

After count dismissal, I grabbed my coat and announced I was headed over to CFS. "See you all later."

"Don't let nobody be stabbing you girl!" Angie laughed.

As I quickly descended the stairs and approached the first-floor center atrium, I signed out for work duty at the desk, and headed out into the cold brisk air. I was eager to be starting this new adventure. After weeks with no designated direction, I was newly energized and confident to be moving forward and attempting to get on with my life again - such as it was.

I hurriedly ran up the steps to CFS, strolled through the front doors and walked back to the rear of the cafeteria. As I stopped at the 3-foot metal swinging doors, I announced to the closest woman working behind the counter that I was here to report to Miss C.

"Miss C! Someone here to see you!" the inmate called as she stepped just inside the small office to announce my presence.

"She'll be right with you," she advised me.

"Ok, thank you."

As I waited patiently for Miss C, I glanced around at the other women behind the cafeteria serving counter. Many were cleaning out huge steam troughs and then filling them with hot steaming water, as others were wiping down trays and placing silverware in the appropriate bins. A few of the women were stirring hot chili in extremely large cooking bins; some were taking huge pans of cornbread out of giant ovens, and others were refilling the fruit and condiment bowls and trays. A few of the women were preparing salads in large plastic bins to be placed into the "cold" section of the serving line, and others were slicing pieces of assorted frozen cream pies. I couldn't help but notice the knives were firmly secured to the wall with flexible, metal cable wires so they could not be removed from the cutting area. I instantly felt an enormous sense of relief. As I continued to watch the women quietly chattering, laughing, and working together, I inhaled the sweet aroma of baking bread and hot soup.

"Friend?" a woman's deep voice suddenly brought me back to the reality of the moment.

"Yes, mam," I promptly responded.

"Come on in. Have a seat," as she motioned me to a chair next to hers in the extremely small office space. I immediately glanced toward the large metal cupboard located against the wall next to the desk, and noticed the doors were securely locked in place with a chain and padlock. Once again, a huge sense of relief filled my being.

"I'm Miss C. That is all you will ever know of my name, so don't ask me. Someday when you go home, and you will, I may see you on the streets, but I will not acknowledge you. That's just my rules. But while you are here, I am your immediate supervisor at this location, and you will respect my word and my decisions. Are we clear?"

"Yes, ma'am," I firmly stated.

"Good. Now that's settled, let's get to work," she declared.

A fairly tall, well-defined and attractive black woman, I would eventually learn that Miss C was a lieutenant within the ranks of the state correctional system. Her short dark curly hair tucked neatly up under a black "military" ball cap with gold lettering, she wore a crisp white short-sleeve shirt, black pleated dress pants with a belt, and black patent leather shoes. Miss C was most likely in her mid-forties. She was somewhat stern, meant business and expected everyone to work hard, share responsibility and be respectful. At the same time, there was a very generous and calming side to her nature. She would laugh and talk freely among the women, always holding true to her values and rules. If someone appeared to be hurting or needed help, she would take them aside and counsel them, providing them with direction and encouragement. On occasion, I would notice her give a few of the inmates a quick side hug, or a pat on the back with an "atta girl!" In time I came to highly respect and admire Miss C for her fortitude, character, and concern for others. And I felt safe around her. I knew she would always protect me from any harm. . . and *knives!*

Tonight, it would be acceptable for me to wear my tennis shoes, however she provided me with orders to pick up work boots at the supply center the following morning. She also gave me a schedule that consisted of 40 hours a week, mostly in the evening until 7:00 pm (or until the kitchen was properly cleaned and we were permitted to leave). She then handed me a hair net and said, "Put this on and let's get you set up with Mr. Y. He'll get you started on the floor tonight and find a position for you to work."

A short, nice-looking Asian man, Mr. Y was also clean-cut, dressed in a military ball hat, white short-sleeve shirt, black dress pants and black shiny shoes. He was a sergeant on the compound and in spite of his small stature, presented an exceptionally large presence. The women liked and respected Mr. Y as well, and were quick to do as he asked of them.

"This is Friend, and she will be working with us," Ms. C introduced me. "If you could get her set up for the dinner shift, that would be great. She'll pick up her work boots tomorrow, so be careful on the floor tonight," she cautioned as she turned her attention back to me. "I'm getting ready to leave for the evening, so Mr. Y will take care of you."

"Friend?" Mr Y questioned.

"Yes, sir," I quickly answered.

"Ok. Let's have you help these ladies get the line set up. We need to be ready in about 20 minutes before serve time."

I followed the lead of others, retrieving food, condiments, and butter slices from the large walk-in refrigerators, as well as placing spoons and forks in the silverware baskets, and stacking trays. Once it was time to place the cooked food out, I helped carry large pans of hot soup and trays of cornbread and position them along the serving line above the steaming hot water-filled bins. During dinner, I was instructed to carry the empty pans back to the sink area for washing, as new pans of food replaced the emptied ones.

In the large dish room, Mr. Johnson was in charge. Now, Mr. Johnson was a different story. A tall and exceptionally large black man, most likely around 325 lbs. or more, Mr. Johnson joked around with the ladies and would sometimes try to get them riled up. Even with a scar-pitted face, a few missing teeth and his substantial weight, he was fairly nice-looking, but it was obvious that Mr. Johnson was insecure in his position of working with the women all day. Though he was strong and robust, the inmates often ignored him and told him to "do it yourself!" as they laughed out loud. Mr. Johnson didn't have a rank other than CO, and the ladies took advantage of that. He was always threating to write them up, but never really did, and they knew it. For the most part they were only playing around, and would do what he asked, but they sure gave him a hard time about it.

After dinner, Mr. Y prepared to leave and told us to do whatever Mr. Johnson asked, without any problems! He soon left for the night, and the mischief began. We were permitted to prepare a plate and eat in the dining area, where everyone was talking and giggling out loud throughout dinner. But soon Mr. Johnson called us back to the kitchen, and I was immediately put to work scrubbing the dirty pans as everyone else cleaned, dried, and put away dishes, pans, and utensils; mopped the floors and wiped down large tray racks, as well as all the counter tops. However, not without Mr. Johnson constantly stating that the pans and racks were not clean enough, the counters needed wiped down better, the floors were still dirty, and to do everything all over again! I could see now why the women gave him a hard time right back, and was beginning to sense more and more what I could only imagine what it might be like to be in the military: do everything over again and again!

Fortunately, however, I was directed with a few of the others out to the dining area to wipe down tables, stack chairs on top of the tables, sweep, mop and roll up the carpet runners. I was exhausted and ready to go back to the unit!

But it was a good night that went by quickly. Once released, I left for my dorm, ready to take a shower and get a restful night's sleep. I eventually crawled into my top bunk, thankful to read a few bible verses and pray with Sofie, and then drift off into a deep and peaceful sleep.

Twas' the Season

She will give birth to a son, and you are to give him the name Jesus, because he will save his people from their sins.
Matthew 2:21

Now the 3rd week of December, most of the women within each unit were making and displaying handmade Christmas decorations, practicing for pageants, rehearsing with the choir, or participating in a variety of other activities well underway for the holiday season. I was becoming more and more depressed, however. This would be the very first Christmas *ever* that I would not be with my family, my children, or my grandchildren. I did not want to participate in any of the activities, nor even think about Christmas this year. Thanksgiving had been hard enough.

I kept as busy as possible with work and writing letters, as well as gathering my visitation information together so I could eventually start having visitors – hopefully within a few weeks. I had received my phone card and had been able to make phone calls to talk with Jennifer and Don, as well as to speak with my older children: Jamie (son), and my daughters, Jodi and Jill. The oldest three lived on their own with their spouses and children, but I wanted desperately to hear their voices, and to *please* have them check in on Jennifer for me.

I wasn't quite sure what was going on at home, as each time I attempted to talk with Don, he seemed to be pulling further and further away from me. He appeared to be very distant and vague about everything I asked him. I truly loved this man with all my heart, and was desperately counting on him for his continued love and encouragement. Now four years into our relationship, he had promised me we would get through this together, and he would stay with me through it all. However, I was becoming concerned that he was losing faith in me.

My main concern, however, was that Jen was okay, and I wanted to make sure she would have a few things under the tree on Christmas morning. I was just sick to my stomach at the thought of not being there for my kids and grandkids. What kind of a mother had I been? It was becoming even more difficult for me to face this horrible transgression I had committed. This was *my* sin, and it wasn't fair to my children, or any of my family, in any way. I had made them a victim of my crime, as well. They had not done anything at all to deserve the pain and suffering of the horrible situation *I* had created. I would have honestly given *anything* to undo my stupid and irresponsible actions. How could I ever make this right - either for my family or my victims?

"Hey, you wanna go downstairs and make some fudge in the microwave?" Sofie interrupted my thoughts.

I had just stepped out of the shower after work and was drying my hair. "Sure, give me a few minutes."

After thinking about it I asked her, "Do you have everything we need? I just got my first pay, but I don't have any chocolate or anything. I don't know what else you might need?"

"Oh, no, I got it. I start saving for this stuff way back. It wouldn't be Christmas without fudge!" she joyfully replied.

Suddenly I remembered that Sofie had not been home with *her* family or young son for over 10 years now. And Angel and Joy were missing Christmas with their *little* kids. I knew I should be thankful that my children were old enough to understand for one year. Not that it made it any easier; and in all my determination and conviction to make things good for my children, I certainly wasn't feeling in charge of anything good right now.

"C'mon! Let's get down there before we have to wait in line for the microwave!" Sofie ordered.

"I'm coming. Let me get my shoes," as I grabbed them from underneath my bunk.

We scrambled downstairs, carrying empty plastic *Ramen*

Noodle bowls, a bag of marshmallows, Nestle's chocolate candy bars, packets of sugar and butter (which were no doubt *donated* by the kitchen), and plastic spoons.

"Don't you worry that we have this sugar and butter out in front of everybody?" I asked as I cautiously looked around.

"Only one you need to worry 'bout is the CO, and 'ol girl not paying one bit attention to us. She too busy reading that *People* magazine. Now, help me unwrap all this stuff. Besides, the rest of it is mine, bought and paid for. You worry too much," Sofie softly scolded me.

The fudge turned out great, and we shared some of it with Cricket, Angel and Tanisha while playing cards that night. I was finding some form of solace and comfort with these ladies. We laughed and joked and made the very best of the situation we were all in together.

Tanisha announced she should be leaving anytime now, and I let her know that I would miss her and wished her well with her new baby when he was born. It would only be two days later when I learned that she had been taken back to her county jail and very possibly would be home for Christmas. Deep inside I knew I would miss this soft-spoken young woman with the very large smile and even larger than life out-of-date glasses. I couldn't deny I felt a small twinge of jealousy, and yet was pleased that at least one of us would be home with their family for Christmas. And what a grand gift for her . . . to know that she would soon be giving birth to a healthy baby boy.

He will be a joy and delight to you, and many will rejoice because of his birth . . .   *Luke 1:14*

December 21st – My 2nd Birthday

If you declare with your mouth, "Jesus is Lord," and believe in your heart that God raised him from the dead, you will be saved. For it is with your heart that you believe and are justified, and it is with your mouth that you profess your faith and are saved. Romans 10:9-10

I was ecstatic and overjoyed that early Saturday morning when it was confirmed I would be permitted to have visitors that day! Although I had initially requested this day to have visitation, I had not received any confirmation until just now. I didn't know who all might be coming, or how many would be permitted to come in; I only knew I was excited to see anyone at all.

Fortunately, I wasn't scheduled to work that day, but I wanted to make the time go by quickly as I was nervous and anxious. I cleaned the room, reorganized my drawers and picked out a sweater (actually the only one I had). Now permitted to have hair ties, I pulled my hair up, and put on a little bit of mascara and blush, the very best I could see in the "toaster-mirror." It was probably not the best I could look, but right then, it was ok. I was just so happy to see my family.

Sofie was working in the library that morning, so I decided to go down and hang out with her for a short while. As I descended the stairs, I walked past a group of women that had gathered in the lobby area to sing Christmas carols and put on a short play.

"I'm a nervous wreck, Sofie," I exclaimed. "Do I look

okay? I don't know what to say. I don't even know who's coming, but it doesn't matter."

"You'll be just fine. Those kids or Don aren't gonna care one bit what you look like right now. They just gonna be so glad to see you," as she tried to console me.

"I know. You're right. You're always right. I'm just nervous. Haven't seen anyone for 10 weeks now. Seems like forever!"

"What time you got visitation?" she asked.

"I think they should be calling me about 12:00 noon. I only get an hour," I answered.

"Yea, you get an hour. But that's good! I'm happy for you." Once again, I had to remind myself that Sofie most likely wasn't going to have any visitors for the holidays.

"Will you get to see your son or anyone at all for Christmas?" I asked her.

"Nah, only one time my Mom and sister brought Clarence to see me at Christmas. That was 'bout 3 years ago. But that's ok. They live so far away and don't have no money to be comin' clear up here to see me. I would rather have them spend the money and get Clarence some gifts under the tree. Sometimes they make a road trip and come see me in the summer. But it's all good," she explained, trying to convince not only me, but herself that it was okay she wouldn't be able to see her family.

"I'm sorry Sofie. I'm gonna go on over and listen to the Christmas carolers until they call me," as I stood up to walk over to the CO's desk to make certain I didn't miss my call.

"Ok, see you later. You have a good visit and don't be so nervous!" Sofie half laughed.

I found a seat close to the CO's desk where I could

watch the seasonal production taking place in the lobby. I was now feeling grateful and had decided that this wasn't such a sad day after all.

"Silent night, Holy night. All is calm, all is bright. 'Round yon Virgin Mother and Child, Holy Infant so tender and mild. Sleep in heavenly peace, Sleep in heavenly peace," I very softly sang to myself along with the carolers.

Thank you, God. Thank you for bringing my family this day. I do believe in you, God, and in your son, Jesus. I really do.

It was about 11:45 am. I continued to listen and sing and thank God. I anxiously watched as the clock hanging on the wall drew closer to 12:00 noon. Eventually the singers left the lobby area, and everyone prepared to go to lunch. I sat patiently as I listened for the CO to let me know the visitation area had called for me to come over. I knew it would only be a matter of minutes now.

The round black clock on the ugly green wall now ticked at 10 minutes past 12:00 pm. Possibly there was some hold-up in the visitation area. This was the first time for my kids or Don to come, so they must have to go through some last-minute paperwork or checklist - or something. But I knew it would be ok very soon. I would still have plenty of time to visit.

It was drawing near to 12:20 pm. I wouldn't move. They would be calling me any minute. I checked with the CO to make certain she had not missed the call. Could she please call over for me and see if there was a problem? Now I was getting really nervous.

"Friend?" I about jumped out of my seat.

"Yes, ma'am?" I excitedly answered. This was it. I could go over now.

"I'm sorry. But you don't have any visitors today," she explained.

No, that couldn't be possible. There had to be a mistake. "Are you sure? Could you please ask them again?" I pleaded with the CO. "I know they would come to see me if they were told they could." I begged her to please check again.

"No, ma'am. You do not have any visitors today. Now go on back to your room or hurry to get some lunch if you want," she instructed me.

This couldn't be happening. I knew my family would come to see me. I didn't understand this at all. I was sick to my stomach with the disappointment and pain of missing my family. I didn't know what could have possibly happened. I ran back up to my room, tears streaming down my face. *Oh God! Why? I don't understand!*

I yanked my blue knit V-neck sweater off and scurried up the ladder to lay on my bunk, buried my face deep within my pillow and sobbed with great sorrow. I couldn't believe this was really taking place. My sin and heartache became a crushing weight. I just wanted to die right then. I couldn't take anymore rejection or disappointment.

"What's going on girl?" Sofie asked as she walked into the room after lunch. "Why aren't you on your visit?"

I raised my head and looked at her with swollen red eyes. "I don't know what happened. I waited and then asked the CO to check for me and she said that I didn't have any visitors today. I don't know what happened!" I began sobbing again.

"Ok, come here," she softly ordered me, "Come down here so we can pray."

I wasn't sure I wanted to do that at all. I wasn't very

happy with God right then. I had just been thanking Him and telling Him how much I believed and loved Him and Jesus. . . and now I had no visitors.

I reluctantly, but obediently, climbed down the ladder and sat on the edge of my lock box while Sofie sat on the edge of her bed. She took my hands into her hands and proceeded to thank God for this day, and that although something had gone wrong, there would most definitely be other days. We prayed for the safety of my family, that nothing bad or harmful had caused them not to be able to come. Possibly they had just not received the notice in time to make the trip. But we thanked Him for the day when they would be able to come again, and to please take away the pain and sorrow of a disappointing day. . . that *a new day* would come, and all of the pain would soon pass.

Then Sofie said something I wasn't expecting or was sure I understood at all. She said "Have you accepted Jesus into your heart? Do you believe that He will save you from all of your sins, and that He is the only way to the Father in heaven?"

I slowly answered, "I believe in Jesus. I believe in God. I'm not sure what you are asking me," rather hesitant that she was going to want me to swear to some kind of belief I really didn't understand.

"Ok, let's read this together," as she pulled out a folded, well worn-out piece of paper from the desk drawer, then walked back to her bunk as she read it out loud to me:

"Have you ever realized there is a God Who knows just where you are? He created you in His image with a special purpose, and He loves you with an everlasting love. Although God loves every person, each of us are born with a sin nature. We are sinners by birth and sinners by choice. Our sin separates us from God and must be paid for. Jesus Christ, God's sinless Son, suffered *our* death on the cross, paying *our* sin debt in full. Christ took the punishment that we deserve. Each person must personally pray and receive Christ by *FAITH*, as our Savior. Just praying a prayer cannot save a person – only ***faith*** in Jesus Christ can save him."

"God's Word says in John 3:16 *For God so loved the world, that He gave His only begotten Son, that whoever believes in him shall not perish but have eternal life.* This was done so that our sins would be forgiven forever."

Sofie sat straight up now. "Do you understand what I am saying?" she asked. "That you must be willing to confess your sin and ask Jesus into your heart, into a personal relationship with Him? Is that what you want to do?" she continued.

At that very moment, I was hurting so bad, I wanted anything to help me, change me, fix me. "Yes, I want to be saved. I want to be a better person. I can't take this crazy and senseless life anymore. I need help. I need Jesus!"

"Ok, come here." Sofie softly instructed me to get on my knees, and to repeat after her. We held hands, closed our eyes and prayed:

"Dear Jesus, I confess to you that I am a sinner. Please forgive me for my sins and thank you for dying on the cross so that my sin may be forgiven. I receive You as my Lord and Savior. Please come into my life and help me to live for you the rest of my life. In the name of Jesus, I pray. Amen."

Right there, in the midst of my pain, my deep sorrow, and my overwhelming need to change my life, I knelt on the cold cement floor of a prison cell, and in all sincerity, gave my life and heart to Jesus Christ that very day. Sofie hugged me afterward and said,

"There! Now you're born again . . . in the spiritual life. Today is your 2nd Birthday! So, we'll have to do something special to celebrate! Ok?"

Through my tears, now of joy, I hugged her back and said "Yes, thank you! Thank you Sofie! You're the best!"

God had sent Sofie ahead of me to that prison cell, to prepare the way for me . . . for my **true** salvation.

The LORD within her is righteous; he does no wrong. Morning by morning he dispenses his justice, and every new day he does not fail . . . Zephaniah 3:5

A New Day

Just at that moment the CO yelled up the stairs. "Friend? Friend! . . . You have a visitor!"

Sofie and I instantly looked at each other in total disbelief.

"What did she just say? I have a visitor? How can that be? It's almost 1:50 pm and visitation is over at 2:00 pm," I asked in shocked excitement.

"Well then I guess you better quit wonderin', put that sweater back on and *git* on over there girl! I told you *a new day* would come – so hurry up now!" Sofie ordered me with a gentle shove.

The Lord is not slow in keeping his promise, as some understand slowness. Instead, he is patient with you, not wanting anyone to perish, but everyone to come to repentance.
2 Peter 3:9

Chapter 5

Visitation

noun: An instance of visiting, coming to see another for social or business reasons; briefly spending time with someone, a place or an occasion. An official visit (as for inspection); temporary custody of or visitation rights. A special dispensation of divine favor or wrath. A severe trial: affliction.

". . . I needed clothes and you clothed me, I was sick and you looked after me, I was in prison and you came to visit me."
Matthew 25-36

The Visit

I all but ran down the winding steps to the CO's desk and signed out of the unit to attend my very first visit. With tears of joy running down my cheeks, and a huge smile of relief, albeit disbelief, on my face, I quickly headed to the "Admin" building where the visitation room was located just inside the main secured entrance of the prison.

As I approached the Visiting Area CO's desk just prior to entering the room, I would be required to sign in for my scheduled visit, be reminded of the rules--no intimate touching, kissing, or otherwise close encounters--and then quickly patted down to ensure I was not carrying in any "illegal" paraphernalia (items to give to my family for possible safe keeping, etc.).

"Ok. Friend. You have 30 minutes to visit," the CO promptly announced.

"Yes ma'am. Thank you!" I was filled with anticipation of who might be seated just inside the room (other than an attorney or other legal counsel, you are not provided any information of who might be there to visit you), what would I say to them; or would I be able to contain my excitement and not break down and cry? Of course, I knew the answer would be *no,* and I began to sob as soon as I peered into the large, although almost empty, visitation area. But it was a joyful cry that burst from me as I looked upon my daughters, Jodi, Jill and Jennifer. With them were two of my grandsons: Christopher, 8 and Jacob, age 3, who ran to greet me with big hugs: "Grandma!" While freshly aware of the rules, I couldn't help but wrap them in hugs. I wasn't about to push them away! Surprisingly, no one said anything to me.

"Oh, Mom. I'm so sorry!" Jodi began to cry as well.

"For what?" I asked as I continued to hug everyone as tightly and quickly as I possibly could. Again, no censure from the CO.

"We got all the way here this morning (a 30-minute drive) and found out we had to have a picture ID. I lost my driver's license a few weeks ago and had to drive all the way back to the BMV to get a new one. That's why we are so late. Then when we got here, they told us visiting hours were almost over. I started crying and telling them we had made the trip two times and had not had a chance to see you for over two months . . . and it was Christmas! The lady asked us to wait a minute and then told us to go ahead and come in here. I'm so sorry!" as she continued to sob.

"Oh, honey. It's ok! Everything is ok. Everything is perfect now. You do not know how happy you have all made me. This is one of the best days of my life! This is my Christmas gift. I love you all so much," I exclaimed.

We all hugged again, and I briefly held the boys on my lap. I asked them how the rest of the family was doing. Jennifer explained that Don had asked her to tell me he would come to visit as soon as he could. I really wasn't surprised and somehow, deep down inside, I had already sensed that he was either pulling away from me, or he couldn't take seeing me in this place. And yet again, it could have just been that he wanted the girls to spend time with me first and then he would come by himself later. Either way, it was just easier for me not to acknowledge what might be going on with him right now. They also explained that Jamie (my son, 27) was having a really hard time, and just couldn't bring himself to come and visit me here. At least not yet. I understood. Although he would probably never admit it, Jamie had always been very emotional, yet reserved with his visible feelings.

We continued to visit, talk, laugh, cry and just enjoy each other's company. I was pleased that Jill had some change with her, as she purchased a Coke and a bag of cheese crackers out of the vending machine for me. Oh, what a day it was! I was totally complete at that moment. *Thank you, God, thank you!*

Soon it was time for everyone to leave and we all hugged again. It almost broke my heart when little Jacob rushed to sit on my lap one last time, put his dimply little hands on my face and very sweetly asked "Grandma, can I stay all night with you tonight?" My heart melted.

"Oh, baby. Grandma's so sorry, but I have to stay here to finish my work. (His parents had explained to him Grandma was at "work".) But when I am all done and get back home, you can come and stay all night with me, ok? It might be a little while, but I promise you can come and visit." I fought to hold back the tears and keep my voice calm.

"But why?" he persisted. His little mind and innocent heart could not understand the situation. And for that, I was so grateful.

"I promise, honey. When Grandma gets home."

I walked with them to the door of the corridor, said our goodbyes and promises of another visit as soon as possible. I watched as they entered the exit area, fixing my eyes upon my precious children for as long as I possibly could. My thoughts were then snapped back to reality as I was directed back to the hallway. "You do understand you are required to undergo a full strip search after each visit, don't you?" the CO inquired.

"No, but it's ok." I was surprised at my new outlook of this otherwise much-dreaded procedure. We stepped inside the bathroom just off the hallway.

"Consider it pure joy, my brothers and sisters, whenever you face trials of many kinds, because you know that the testing of your **faith** *produces perseverance."* James 1:2-3

The Visitation

At that time Mary got ready and hurried to a town in the country of Judea, where she entered Zechariah's home and greeted Elizabeth. When Elizabeth heard Mary's greeting, the baby leaped in her womb, and Elizabeth was filled with the Holy Spirit. In a loud voice she exclaimed: "Blessed are you among women and blessed is the child you will bear! But why am I so favored, that the mother of my Lord should come to visit me? As soon as the sound of your greeting reached my ears, the baby in my womb leaped for joy. Blessed is she who has believed that the Lord would fulfill his promises to her!" Luke 1:39-45

Now after Jesus was born in Bethlehem of Judea in the days of Herod the king, behold, wise men from the East came to Jerusalem, saying "Where is He who has been born King of the Jews? For we have seen His star in the East and have come to worship Him."   *Matthew 2:1-2*

It was Christmas Eve. I laid upon the top bunk with my arms crossed behind my head, a thin white blanket and my coat covering me from head to toe, and my eyes fixed upon the ceiling approximately 4-feet above me.

My cellmates were downstairs celebrating with the other ladies, or possibly on the phone with their loved ones. The sounds of singing, laughing, music playing; and the intermittent buzz of the microwave proclaiming it had completed its cycle, as well as the aroma of freshly popped popcorn, melting chocolate and marshmallows, and chicken flavored *Ramen* noodles, drifted up to the 2nd floor and down the hallways.

This night was no different than any other night in jail, however. There were always those Inmates who had to fight, swear and scream at each other as loudly as possible; and otherwise make everyone around them as miserable as they were. I could hear the footsteps of the CO quickly running up the open stairs and down the hall to see what sort of mischief was taking place now. *Thank you for my safe and quiet room, God.*

I let my mind drift back to happier days, to Christmas Eves "magical" with the anticipation and excitement of family gatherings and events that would unfold over the next few days.

As a small child, upon leaving the Christmas Eve ritual of 5:00 pm Mass with my large family, I would take my seat in the back of our sizable 1960, dull-yellow Mercury station wagon, packed high with gifts, cookies, babies, and kids (there were 7, eventually 8 of us), press my nose up against the cold glass of the side window and search for the North Star. I would recall the stories Mammy had told me about the three Wise Men who had followed the star that would lead them to the manger; and I just knew that if we followed it, it would certainly lead us to the baby Jesus!

But we always ended up at Grandma & Grandpa Braxton's house where we would have a great time with our cousins, enjoy a huge buffet set up of ham and turkey sandwiches, salads, jellos, chips, veggie and fruit trays, and of course homemade Christmas cookies and candies. We would open gifts, play games, and at the end of the evening eventually prepare to leave for home where we would soon be tucked away in our beds where visions of sugar plums . . . but mostly of new toys under the Christmas tree . . . would dance in our heads.

As my mind continued to wander, I turned over on my side, pulled the covers up tighter around my neck, and faced the cement wall. I couldn't help but wonder where everyone was on this special evening. Had my parents and some of my siblings enjoyed Christmas Eve dinner together, and were now preparing to go to Midnight Mass? Were all my children and grandchildren gathering at Jodi's house to eat, open gifts and celebrate together as we had always done? Would Don be at the VFW hall drinking with his friends? He would not be with his family tonight as he had always gone to his mother's house to visit on Christmas Day.

He had surprised me with a beautiful Christmas card, writing how very sorry he was that he had not come to visit with me yet, and that he really did love me with all of his heart. He was just so heartsick right now and missed me terribly. He said we would get though all of this somehow. That's all I needed to hear. He put $40 on my books and explained that he was giving Jennifer $100 to go shopping. (He also explained Jill had told him their Dad had given them money to go shopping for Jennifer to ensure she would have gifts under the tree.) My heart was at peace now.

This year Christmas Eve was very different from years past. It was missing all those happy feelings and activities, but tonight there was a much deeper experience of Christ's birth than I had ever known. I reached under my pillow where I kept my bible and began to read again the story of the birth of the baby Jesus. Other than the childhood stories I had been taught of the baby Jesus who was born in a manger, and of all the shepherd boys and kings from other countries who came to visit Him; this was the first year I had ever *read* this amazing story of the miracle birth of our Savior. I realized now more than ever that this man, the son of God, was not only a very real person; but now His spirit actually did live within my heart.

Although not worthy in any way, I almost felt as Mary and Elizabeth might have felt when they had been honored and blessed with the visit of the angel, and the spirit of God was upon them. Although only having prayed with Sofie a few days earlier, at that very moment I truly sensed in my heart that God had sent His angel to tell *me* that I had been forgiven, and that He loved me despite all my sins.

I certainly had not done anything in any way to deserve His mercy and grace, and yet there it was: His unconditional love and forgiveness. . . for me, a horrible sinner. I closed my eyes and felt His loving arms surround me with peace and comfort. I truly felt His presence . . . He had come to visit me in that prison cell on Christmas Eve. Very softly the tears of gratitude and undeserved compassion rolled down my cheeks onto my pillow. I realized now that the "magical" Christmas feeling inside the pit of my stomach had now been replaced with that of a "miraculous" and calming spirit deep within me.

I only want to please you Lord. I only want you to love me and make me be a better person. Please take away all the sinful thoughts, ways. . . and all that is evil in my life, Lord.

Christmas Day

But the angel said to them, "Do not be afraid. I bring you good news that will cause great joy for all the people. Today in the town of David a Savior has been born to you; he is the Messiah, the Lord. This will be a sign to you: You will find a baby wrapped in cloths and lying in a manger." Suddenly a great company of the heavenly host appeared with the angel, praising God and saying, "Glory to God in the highest heaven, and on earth peace to those on whom his favor rests."

Luke 2:10-14

The next morning was truly a new day. "Good morning! Merry Christmas!" I exclaimed as I scampered out of bed and got ready to go to breakfast with Sofie and Angel for the first time since I had been there. I didn't usually eat breakfast, but this morning we enjoyed sausage patties, warm pancakes with butter and syrup, and orange juice. What a delicious treat for sure!

After breakfast we hung out in the game room and talked with Cricket and a few other inmates I had briefly met before: Helen and Tonya. These ladies shared a 2-person room together on the first floor. Both inmates were serving time for grand theft.

A middle-aged white woman with short but stylish dark brown hair with gray streaks peeking through, Helen was most likely in her mid-forties. She was especially attractive and obviously otherwise well-off financially. She talked of her loving husband, their huge house and her Corvettes. She proudly showed us photos of the "babies" she longed to hold again: two little white adorable Maltese dogs that she loved and missed terribly. I would also come to learn this was now her third conviction and time spent in prison. Now drawing closer to her final release date, she had been serving eight years of this particular sentence. Curiosity got the best of me, and I couldn't help but ask, "And your husband stays with you through all of this?"

"Well, of course he does! He loves me. He just stays at home all the time and takes care of the dogs for me. He'll never leave me. He's got it made. *I* take care of *him*. He just goes to the country club and golfs all the time."

I was completely perplexed by that. Obviously, this was a way of life for them. I couldn't help but notice the new chic and soft leather loafers she had on; the beautiful, although very small diamond stud earrings, or the gold watch she was wearing. Certainly, the jewelry couldn't be real. But what did I know? This place was certainly a lot more lenient and permissive than Maryswood!

Tonya was much younger, most likely in her upper twenties. A beautiful and vivacious white girl, she had long dark shiny hair, pulled up into a ponytail. An energetic and playful spirit, I also noticed she was wearing a pair of name brand tennis shoes, and a silver necklace of a heart outlined with what I was sure had to be cubic zirconia. There was no way that necklace had real diamonds in it! I didn't think it would even be possible to possess such jewelry within the compound. Other than a watch, as far as I knew, no one could keep any jewelry, most likely due to possible theft, liability or "use as a weapon" motive. I was delighted when Angel finally asked, "I love your necklace. Is that new?"

Rats! Why couldn't she have asked if they were *real*? Hoping Tonya would give up the true identity of the stones, I was disappointed when she only replied "Yes, this is my Christmas gift from Helen! Isn't it gorgeous?" I still didn't know what to believe.

My curiosity killing me regarding this relationship, like that of an impatient cat; when we were alone later, I asked my cellmates about it. Sofie explained, "Aw, y'know, Helen *takes care* of Tonya," and Angel added with a wink, "Yeah, she's her *girl!* Helen buys her all kinds of expensive gifts and scored her a job with her on the outside - in the warehouse office!"

"What do you mean she is her "girl"? And how do they get to work on the outside?" I was more curious than ever.

"Girl, don't you know anything at all? These women up in here been without their lover all this time. Most of them be with each other so they don't be so lonely. And they a part of only eight inmates on the whole compound who get to go on the outside every day for they job," Angel explained.

I guess I really did know that a lot of the women in here were living a much different lifestyle within the confines of these walls than what they normally would on the outside. Most of them were just very good about covering it up, unlike those at Maryswood where huge open dorms and bathrooms proved to be of no consequence to those indulging in an open relationship.

"Outside, like out in the streets? How in the heck does that happen?" I was in shock that there was such an opportunity.

"Yeah, and someday I'm gonna get to go out to work in the streets. You watch, you'll see!" Angel continued. She really didn't answer my question, but I believed this had to be an exceptional possibility that I would never get the privilege to have.

I called all my kids and grandsons later that afternoon. Everyone had a good Christmas day and had worked hard to make it as special as possible. The girls made cut-out cookies and potato candy just like we had always done, and Jamie made the ham loaf. Bless his heart, he did try, but said he burned it a little. Everyone else said it was fine. I was so proud of them. They all promised they would come to visit with me again in a few weeks.

Later I tried to call Don, but knew he was out of town visiting with his mother and siblings for the day, so I would try to call him later. I also called my parents' house, but when my father answered the phone, he very briefly and coldly said, "Merry Christmas" and then immediately handed the phone to my Mom. It was a very awkward and short conversation with both parents. I knew they were upset with me and my children because they had decided not to visit with their grandparents this year. There was just too much pain and turmoil going on between everyone right now. But at this point I truly was not concerned about it. It certainly wouldn't be the first time in my life that my parents would cut off or not talk to someone within the (entire) family because they did not agree with or were upset with a family member for some (and most usually minor) reason. But I noticed what would have once caused me anxiety didn't torment me now. I was getting better and stronger within my heart and soul with each day. I knew to put my faith in God right now, not my parents.

*But God has proven his **faith**fulness in my weakness. "And the God of all grace who called you to his eternal glory in Christ, after you have suffered a little while, will himself restore you and make you strong, firm, and steadfast. All power to Him forever! Amen."*   *1 Peter 5:10-11*

January 2000 - Y2K

The onset of New Year's Eve filled the entire institution with fear and foolish rumors that the world would surely come to an end that very night at the stroke of midnight. The only thing I could think was that at least I wouldn't have to try to find a job now - now that I would have a felony record!

There were indeed stories on the news of people stockpiling cans of food, gallons of water, bedding, toiletries, flashlights, radios, weapons, etc. Word on the "prison walk" was that a once notable Christian evangelist had proclaimed the Lord appeared to him in a vision and told him that unless his followers sent his ministry one-million dollars by midnight, he would surely be put to death. Now I was just a brand-new believer, but I had already heard something similar to this very story several years prior and knew by this time not to believe everything these women were attempting to stir up. It appeared that for some inmates, anything to create drama and panic was what seemed to falsely provide a sense of "power" or authority over others. I had to chuckle to myself as this reminded me of the old fable of "Chicken Little" who was running around in hysterics that the sky was falling, and most certainly the end of the world was upon them!

I did understand that "Y2K" was a legitimate "scare" of computer users and programmers who feared that computers would stop working at midnight of December 31, 1999. When the original computer programs were created in the 1960's, engineers only used a two-digit code for the year, and as the new Millennium approached, computer experts realized that the original software would recognize "00" as 1900 instead of the year 2000. This posed a very real threat to many institutions such as insurance companies, hospitals, government departments and banks that relied on computers to provide accurate time and date.

Anxiety spread across the world as people feared that computer systems would shut down and throw the world into chaos. As a result, stock prices of banks dropped in value as the year 2000 neared. There were rumors that planes would drop from the sky when clocks turned to midnight. Fortunately, the "year 2000" problem was handled by creating new software programs that saved dates as four digits instead of the two digits previously used.

We somehow managed to live through Y2K, only to succumb to three days of no heat whatsoever on the entire campus. Something had happened to the heating systems, and although almost a week after the initial scare of doom and gloom, a lot of the women believed it was somehow due to the failure of a "computerized" heating system. Many were convinced we would surely freeze to death!

Layered in long underwear, long sleeve shirts, sweaters, 2-pair of socks and pants, winter coats, and covered with our blankets wherever we went within the unit, it was becoming more and more intolerable each day. Fortunately for me, I had been promoted to "Cook", working 15-hour shifts in the kitchen (3 days a week) where I could at least be close to the ovens and stove tops for the majority of the day.

During the night I would stay in bed completely clothed and covered up, although even that proved to be a nightmare. Explained to us the cold air must be left on in the units because the temperature of this air was at least in the 30's and 40's, unlike the 20-degree and below weather outside; therefore, they would not shut down the continuous cold air flow gusting through the vents. Nothing but absolute frigid air would blow directly on me and Joy on the top bunks - so we were especially freezing! We kept stuffing the vents with towels to stop the cold air flow. But the CO would always make us take out the towels. We were both coughing and sniffling the entire time. Finally, Joy had had enough. I never heard her get so angry as when she yelled at the CO that we couldn't take it anymore.

"Do you *NOT* understand how *"f...ing"* cold it is in here?" she shrieked one night when the CO came in for 10:00 pm count, and we were ordered once again to remove the towels.

Swearing at a CO, and especially during *count* when there was to be absolutely no talking what-so-ever, was an outright insubordination offense punishable by time in the "hole".

"Landis! Report to me downstairs immediately after count! Understood?" she demanded.

With our eyes wide open and holding our breath at what Joy might say next - she quietly answered, "Yes ma'am," yet with a distinct and stubborn edge to her voice.

She was still full of rage however, and as soon as the CO stepped out of the room, she whispered under her breath that maybe at least it would be warmer in the hole. She really didn't care; she just couldn't take it anymore.

Of course, Angel had to add her 2 cents and quietly start snickering about the whole episode. "Shut up Angel!" Sofie sternly shut her down in a whispered voice.

Fortunately, or maybe unfortunately for her, Joy did not have to go to the hole, and the CO would not write her up under the circumstances; but she did receive a very severe tongue-lashing. Possibly her depressive attitude and strong stance had helped however, as the heat was restored early the following morning.

> *He looked around at them in anger and, deeply distressed at their stubborn hearts, said to the man, "Stretch out your hand." He stretched it, and his hand was completely restored.*
>
> Mark 3:5

The Red Sea

Although mid-January, I continued to try to walk on the "Walk-Jog" everyday if I could possibly stand the cold. But eventually it became so frigid, and the asphalt so deeply snow-covered, that I was forced to halt my daily walks. I missed this time alone each day. This was my time to think to myself, reflect upon my past, talk to God, pray, and just spend time with Him. I had to resort to spending this time, as well as reading the Bible and other books, bundled up in my bunk.

"Friend!" Miss C summoned me to come to her office. I was at work, in the middle of preparing for lunch that day.

"You need to report to the Chaplain's office. It's not an emergency or anything like that. But she needs to see you. Go ahead and sign out and then come right back here."

"Yes ma'am. Thank you."

I couldn't imagine what on earth the Chaplain would want to see me about and was surprised when I arrived at her office and told that I had received a Bible from my parents as a Christmas gift. However, Chaplain Burnside went on to explain that I would not be permitted to keep it, as it had been mailed directly from their home address and would have to be returned to them. Receiving books, posters, magazines, etc. from the outside was not permitted. Regardless, the Chaplain then surprised me with my own full-version bible containing both the Old and New Testaments. Until now, I had still been reading from my "Good News" bible (containing New Testament only). This was yet another visitation!

"The Word became flesh and dwelt among us. . ."John 1:14

On my days off or late in the evening, I enjoyed reading my new bible and all about the creation of the earth and the story of Adam and Eve, the account of Noah and the flood, as well as many other stories that I had never even heard of. I didn't know who Abraham and Sarah, Isaac and Rebekah, or Joseph and his brothers were. This was all new to me. I wanted to know the stories of these people of God. Why would God send angels of prophets to speak directly to them, to listen to their fears and thoughts; correct them when they had sinned, provide them with gifts and blessings, save them from harm, and drive out their enemies? *Well . . . I guess because that is what a loving Father would do.*

And yet, I sovereignly wondered to myself - *God created all men? Then why were there enemies? Why did people make fun of Noah when he was building the ark? Could it be possible that some men and nationalities didn't believe in God, or possibly believe they didn't need Him; or could do everything on their own? Did they believe they didn't need to pray, or ask God for His help? . . . I guess like when I said I could do all of this on my own? That I would be "in charge" of my life? Yeah, and how was that working out for me? I was still in prison, and I sure wasn't going anywhere anytime soon.*

One night I was lying in bed and reading about God sending the Israelites out of Egypt, so they would no longer be slaves to the Egyptians. He was providing them a way out to possess their own land, and to establish their own nation. Fleeing from the Egyptians, who were close on their heels and determined to bring them back into slavery, the Israelites came upon the mighty Red Sea. Trapped at this raging water with nowhere to turn, they cried out in fear and . . .

They said to Moses, "Was it because there were no graves in Egypt that you brought us to the desert to die? What have you done to us by bringing us out of Egypt?"

And the Lord said to Moses:

". . . lift up they rod and stretch out thy hand over the sea and divide it: and the children of Israel shall go on dry ground through the midst of the sea."   *Exodus 14:11 &16*

The Israelites then crossed over safely, and the Egyptian soldiers all perished as God closed the violent and furious waters back over them.

I shot straight up off that bunk. "Sofie! Did you know that God parted the Red Sea for the Israelites? I didn't know that! If God had parted the Red Sea for me, I would have believed in Him!" I was thrilled to think that God really, really did perform actual miracles for people.

"*Girl!* What are you talkin' 'bout? You didn't know that? You kidding right?" she retorted.

"Well, I remember seeing a black and white movie once when I was really little that showed something like that. But

I just thought it was Hollywood. You know like Hercules or Godzilla or something," I sheepishly answered. Maybe I should have known. I was still so confused about what was real and what I didn't understand.

"Listen. You believe that God is real, don't you?" Sofie questioned me.

"Yes, but I didn't know things could really happen like that . . . . I mean I've never seen a huge river just open up and let people pass through it! Or if those things really did happen, that was just for those people. Not for us."

"So, what makes you think that God only answered *their* prayers, or that God is not the same God He Is today that He was then?" Sofie challenged me again.

Embarrassed, I answered, "I don't know. Because He didn't provide me the money that I needed, or make all of the bad things go away, or make me be a good person, or that I could have a good life for my kids . . . all of the things that I prayed for." I tried to reason . . . and yet at that moment I also realized I was blaming God for my terrible life and *for all the choices that I had made.*

"So, all them things you told me 'bout God talking to you and telling you to go home and tell your family and not kill *youself,* and then getting to go home after you were sentenced to prison so you could tell your family and spend the weekend with them; and how God protected you from that girl Peaches from killin' you when you still at Maryswood, and how you asked for cellmates who would pray and read the bible and not cuss all the time," . . . she rattled off, her voice rising, "You don't think God heard your prayers and answered them? THAT was a miracle, girl! God *has* parted the Red Sea for you, over and over again! What part do you not understand?"

I was humbled . . . and ashamed. Yes . . . I did know that God had saved my life and talked to me when I was driving in the car that day . . . the day I tried to kill myself.

Yes, I did know that God had let me go home before turning myself in at the jail, and how He had saved me from being murdered at Marywood.

Sofie's voice calmed. "Do you believe that God loves you?"

"Yes, yes I do. You're right. I do know that God has parted the Red Sea for me, and I just didn't realize it," I softly answered with my head down. I felt ashamed that I didn't really appreciate and see what God was doing for me right now. How many other times had He probably tried to tell me things, but I just wouldn't listen?

. . . The day God visits you has come, the day your watchmen sound the alarm. Now is the time of your confusion.

Micah 7:4

The Final Visit

Almost every weekend after that, I had visitation with someone. For the most part, it was my oldest daughter Jodi who made the 30-minute drive each way to visit with me, but someone was always there.

A few weeks after Christmas, Don finally came to see me. I was surprised, but so happy that he had a big smile on his face when I first entered the room. He started to reach for me, but I caught the look of the CO and knew we could not hug. I apologized but sat across from him and we held hands for a short while.

"I'm sorry it has taken me this long. I really have been wanting to see you. It's just been really hard. I miss you so much," he said as a few tears came to his eyes. "I do feel much better now," he whispered.

We talked and got caught up on a lot of things. He said Jennifer had been cooperative and they were getting along, but he worried that it wasn't right that she should stay with him at our small apartment.

"Don, that is her home. You know she has no place else to go. I completely trust you. You need to stop worrying about what everyone else thinks right now. Or is there something I should know that you're not telling me? *Should I be worried?*"

"No! Not at all. I just don't think it's right, that's all. And you know she is so independent. I don't have time to keep worrying about where she is, or who she is with all the time."

"She told me she leaves you notes about where she is. Is she not doing that?"

"Yeah, she leaves me notes, but I can't be tracking her down all the time," he continued.

"I know . . . I understand, and I really am so sorry. I cannot even begin to tell you how much I appreciate you doing this for me. . . for *us*. I really don't know what I would do without you right now. Please understand that I need you to be strong for me."

With sincere sorrow for all that I had caused, I let the tears fall from my cheeks. I truly loved and appreciated this man for all that he was doing to try to hold things together for us through everything. He didn't deserve any of this. All of the pain, confusion, fear, loneliness, and heartbreak that I had placed on him and my family, was like a heavy rock crushing my heart. I couldn't even begin to grasp how hard this was for him.

Visitation hour now over, we stood across from each other, intensely desiring to just hold each other in comfort, but knew it was forbidden. We grasped hands tightly, but briefly as he promised he would visit again soon. Don's visit assured me I would somehow get through the months ahead. I just needed to know the people I loved would stand beside me.

Don kept his promise and came again in a few weeks. He seemed a little different this time. More distant than before. I felt he was struggling more inside than I could read on his face.

"I have good news, I think," I tried to lift the tension in the air.

"Oh yeah, what's that?" he asked.

"I received a letter stating that I'm eligible to go before the parole board in February. I'm surprised because I have a one-year mandatory sentence and didn't think that could be possible. But the letter says this hearing will determine if I can be allowed to go to a half-way house sometime in June to serve the rest of my sentence there. I'll have to go to classes, look for a job, but then eventually be allowed to come home for weekend visits! Can you believe it?" I exclaimed. "I'll have to have you, or the girls bring me regular street clothes and my things when I get transferred over. But we can figure all that out later. I'm just so excited that I can leave here in

June and then get to come home for visits! We can do this honey. It'll be much better soon! I promise!"

"Where will the half-way house be?" he asked with a curious, although somewhat undeterred look upon his face.

"I'm not sure, but I do know it will either be here in this town, or possibly even closer to home."

"Well, that's great, honey. I'm really happy for you. I hope that works out for you."

I was confused. He's happy for *me?* Like this was just for me now, not for *us*. But I didn't dare ask him. I told myself he just needed more time to work through everything, and it would all be over before we know it.

A few weeks later on a Tuesday, I was working in the kitchen when I heard Miss C call me.

"Friend? You got a visitor!" I was surprised that I would be permitted to have visitation privileges while I was working.

"I can have a visitor now?"

"Girl, you can have a visitor anytime. As long as they come during visitation hours, we gotta let you see them," Miss C explained.

"Oh, okay, great!" I said and then realized how horrible I must look, my hair pulled up into a hair net, a huge dirty white apron wrapped around my body, and those ugly black work boots, did absolutely nothing for me at all. I tried to wipe off my face all the sweat and grease of working at the stoves all day. *Who could possibly be visiting me?* I grabbed my coat and headed for the visitation area. The cool air between the buildings felt good on my face.

When I entered the visiting room, it was Don. He was smiling and looked so happy!

"Oh, my goodness. What are you doing here today?" I asked. "I didn't know you were coming. I look terrible!" as I tried to smooth back my hair and press down my apron. I was a "hot mess" as Angel would say all the time.

"No, you look just fine. But I had to come to see you today. I took the day off work so I could come."

I was flustered, but so pleased that he really wanted to see me that bad. *He must realize we're going to get through this and be okay now!*

"Everything's going to be okay, honey. I promise you. I was really worried for a while, and I have to be honest with you that I didn't know if we were going to make it. But now I know we are, and I promise you I'm not going to leave you."

I realized right then that he really had been contemplating leaving me. I guess I knew he was struggling, but I never imagined that he would actually leave me. *Well . . . at least it's a positive that he's come to this realization.*

He went on to tell me that he had gone out to dinner and to the comedy club with a friend, his daughter and her husband the night before, and that was when it struck him that he truly loved me.

"I can't leave you, Nan. I just can't. I can't do this to you. I can't do this to us," he continued.

I was shocked this had even crossed his mind. We had been together for over four years and had been through a lot of difficulties like any couple, but the thought of ending our relationship had never occurred to me. I somehow maintained my composure, but I wasn't sure whether to be happy or sad at that moment. . . and I was definitely afraid to ask who the "friend" was that went to dinner with them.

He was excited that I had prepared my acknowledgment and defense to present to the parole board that was scheduled in a few weeks. We were both eager to just put all of this behind us as soon as we could. We continued to talk awhile longer, then said our goodbyes with promises that everything was going to work out.

I could not know this would be the last time Don would ever come to see me again. This would be his final visit.

"Be strong and courageous. Do not be afraid or terrified because of them, for the LORD your God goes with you; he will never leave you nor forsake you."   *Deuteronomy 31:6*

CHAPTER 6

❧ *Devastation* ❧

n: the state or fact of being brought to ruin or desolation by violent action, such as war: being reduced to chaos, disorder, or helplessness: overwhelmed by grief; rendered nonexistent, useless; mentally or physically unsound.

"Surely, God, you have worn me out, you have devastated my entire household."   Job 16:7

Goals and Dreams

The first week of February, and I relished the opportunity to mark off yet another month, with now only nine months remaining until my final release date. *They* tell you not to count down your days when you are in prison, but for me it was a huge comfort to be able to mark off each and every date. I was determined to get through this, and I was finding strength day by day in this place of desolation and despair.

I began my GOALS[1] class that same week. This course was designed to help us establish short- and long-term goals for our lives. Miss C taught this session on Monday nights, and I was encouraged by her continued support and reassurance that we could excel at whatever we put our

---

[1] *Gaining Opportunities And Living Skills*
Jack Canfield; Copyright 1989

minds to. Initially I didn't believe I could even create goals for myself. After all, what kind of a future could I possibly have to look forward to?

I was convinced I would never be able to find any kind of decent job or make any kind of a life for myself or my family again. Regardless of our doubts, however, we were urged to think about possible and different solutions - like going back to school; either GEO classes to obtain a high school degree, or to actually attend college courses that were made available here at the facility from a notable, near-by college campus. Eventually, I would find myself beginning to wonder, *what if*? What if I could go back to school, get a decent job, or feel confident about myself again? To me, this was a very big *what if*?

I was a freshman in high school when I first began poring over college brochures that I had picked up in the high school guidance counselor's office. I had always excelled in school and dreamed of the day I could be a college student, until one day when my father and my (maternal) grandmother got into quite a heated argument over whether I should be able to pursue a higher education. She even went so far as to say she would pay the tuition if that was the problem. Yep, she went there - and that certainly did not go over well!

My father had always made it clear that he did not support me in my quest to go to college. This would be a privilege that only my five brothers would ever have. Regardless, I stopped by the College Dean's office the following morning and made the request to apply for an admissions test. I completed the paperwork and returned it in that same afternoon, understanding that I would be notified of the date and time for the exam.

Somehow, I did feel a new confidence that day.

The following week I attended my first class of the "Theft" program. Every Thursday night Chaplain Burnside taught this class designed to help those who had committed any crime of theft, embezzlement, passing bad checks, insurance fraud, or any other type of misappropriation of monetary crimes. Initially, I dreaded these sessions as well, believing that it would only make me feel even more ashamed and despised than I already felt.

However, we were not only asked very pointed questions regarding our specific crime: who, what, where, when (and how many times) did you commit your crime? - but we would delve into the very real reasons of *why*? We were required to write essays on each topic, revealing details and being specific about the motives. We had open discussions about what we did and why we did it; and what were our feelings about those decisions now? We were forced to face these issues head on, as well as to distinguish and recognize within our hearts, the damage we had created for our victims, ourselves, and our families.

Chaplain Burnside backed up a lot of our discussion with biblical verses and teachings, as well. She did not create an atmosphere of accusation, disgust or hostility. Nor did she permit us to think that what we had done was permissible in any way. What she did do, was to give us the opportunity to openly confess the very real issues plaguing us. Her lessons fostered hope, forgiveness and possibility . . . *even for a wretch like me.* I would soon learn to welcome and appreciate this time of honesty and reconciliation.

My Bible study classes would soon begin - taught by a woman, who was a Pentecostal minister at that! *Oh, my goodness - my mother would be in total shock and sternly warn me not to listen to these people who were obviously a religious cult!*

I was pleased however to learn more about the many stories of the Bible. We not only read the passages but discussed them in detail and learned about these people of Biblical times - their (our) heritage, customs, beliefs, sin offerings - and the promise of a Messiah who would one day come to earth to deliver the people from their sins.

For our homework one evening, the minister asked us to look up our favorite verse, memorize it, and be prepared to discuss why it was important to us. I realized that I didn't have a favorite verse. I was at a loss regarding the assignment but determined I would sincerely spend time and search my heart for the precise verse that spoke to me. I eventually decided on Hebrews 11:1:

*Now **faith** is the substance of things hoped for, the evidence of things not seen.*

I knew I needed to understand how to have faith - how to trust, love, forgive and believe again when there were so many wicked things of the world around me that I had no control over. How do you truly have faith when you realize that lies, deceit, corruption and evil are so rampart and a way of life for so many in this realm of which we live? And yet, how could I ever believe that anything could be ever possible for me again, if I didn't have faith?

Okay . . . I had to figure this out - what was faith? It was something that I couldn't see, touch, feel or even explain. It was my innermost belief that God was real, that He loved me, and that I could trust Him; although I could not see or feel Him in the flesh, as humans understand "real" to be.

I stared at the table in front of me. I understood it was real. I could see it, touch it, feel it. I knew it was made of dark wood, had 4 legs, and that if I ran into it, it could possibly injure me. I knew I could count on this table to be strong, sturdy and always be there when I came into the room. I could use it every day to eat on, to fill out paperwork or write letters home; read, play games, or design pretty cards. I counted on this table to be there for me when I needed it. I had a kind of *faith* in the table.

I also realized I had faith that if I turned on the light switch, the lights would come on, although I had absolutely no idea how electricity even works (that in itself is a miracle to me). I did *not* know how my car ran, how the TV can display movies, music, the news and weather through the airwaves, or how a camera can take pictures of precious memories of my children. I knew however, that I trusted and believed that most every time I would use these items, they would work! (Or if not, they could be repaired or replaced.) I seemed to have more faith in man-made, tangible items than I did in God.

I understood that I needed to honestly believe that not only does God exist - but to know that He loves me, He hears my prayers, He knows my pain and suffering, and the desires of my heart. He knows when I am weak, and when I need help. I was beginning to understand that faith makes us stronger, braver, better. It was a trust that I had to develop, just as that of an infant first crawling, and then learning to walk.

I began to understand that God was literally revealing so many things to me; and why He had "opened the Red Sea" for me. I had not trusted anyone for so long, and had built a wall of protection around me; truly believing that if I, and only those I would allow in, could dwell safely within the walls of my castle, no one could ever hurt me, lie to me, cheat on me, or take anything away from me again.

God knew I needed to "see" these things for myself. Just as Jesus instantly healed the man who had been blind from birth:. . .

"Neither this man nor his parents sinned," said Jesus, "but this happened so that the works of God might be displayed in him.   *John 9:3*

- Or just as Jesus performed multiple miracles so that the people would believe and have FAITH that Jesus was who He said he was:

. . . At that very time Jesus cured many who had diseases, sicknesses, and evil spirits, and gave sight to many who were blind.   *Luke 7:21*

. . . And a great crowd of people followed him because they saw the signs he had performed by healing the sick.   *John 6:2*

I knew now that I did not have to fight this battle by myself anymore. I also understood that God had not "sent" me to prison - I had accomplished that all of my own accord, through many bad decisions and lies. But He did *allow* me to come to this place of solitude and isolation in order that He could have my 100% attention to seek Him, learn about Him, trust Him, and love Him. If I had still been on the outside, I wouldn't have taken the time to want to know Him, or how to change my life. But locked within these walls, I could no longer worry about the matters of the outside world. This time was set aside for *me*.

"Who is this that obscures my plans without knowledge?" Surely, I spoke of things I did not understand, things too wonderful for me to know."   Job 42:3

Valentine Cookies and Bingo

Walking back to my unit from the library that Tuesday afternoon, I passed by one of the larger meeting rooms located within the Administration building. There were signs posted along the walls with large, bright red magic-marker lettering:

Bible Bingo!
Tonight 6:00 pm – 8:00 pm
Prizes for Everyone!

I peeked just inside the door at a long table displaying all types of the more expensive and sweet-smelling soaps and shampoos, as well as lip balms, hair combs, scrunchies, candies and various snacks wrapped up in clear gift bags with colorful bows. However, my attention was drawn to the homemade Valentine heart-shaped sugar cookies covered with various shades of red, white and pink powdered sugar icings and sprinkles; two of each placed within individual clear baggies and tied with red ribbons. I knew right then I had to get Sofie to come back with me and win some of those cookies!

"Sofie! You have to go with me to the Admin building

tonight, and win some Valentine cookies!" I called out as I entered the door to our cell.

Sofie was lying on her bunk, taking a brief nap. "What are you talkin' bout girl?" she slowly answered without turning over. I am sure she just wanted me to go away and let her sleep.

I explained in detail all of the exceptional gifts we could possibly win at Bingo. She wasn't nearly as excited to go as I was, but reluctantly said "Ok, ok. Just let me get some sleep before count and I'll go over with you after supper."

Immediately upon finishing our fried chicken, potatoes, and biscuits, and we hurriedly scrambled over to the Admin building and joined the long line of women already forming outside the door to enter the special event.

"Dang it, I knew we should have skipped out on dinner. No way all these women already done and over here before we are!" I complained just like a *seasoned* inmate now!

"Well, no way I was passing up on fried chicken and taters either! Quit frettin'. You gonna git in," Sofie complained right back at me.

"Ok, I know. Thank you for coming with me. Hopefully we won't have to stand out in the cold too much longer," as we pulled our hoodies tight against the wind.

Eventually we made our way inside and waited approximately 20 minutes as everyone was given the opportunity to play at least two games. I could just taste those sugar cookies with each passing moment and smell the peach scented *Caress* soap bars the closer we drew to the door. Eventually we were permitted to enter the room and directed to two empty seats.

After we took our places, it was explained that tonight

everyone was a winner! If you actually won a game, you would be permitted to pick out your own prize, but if you did not win a "Bingo", you would still be provided a gift by one of the volunteers as you left the room. *Ok, that was alright - I didn't care how I got a bag of those cookies! It would still be fun trying.*

As we finished our allotted two games, neither Sofie nor I actually scored a winning game, but we eagerly proceeded to the doorway to receive our prizes. The moment was here! I would soon have those delicious and beautiful cookies in my hands! As I slowly approached the ladies waiting just outside the doors, I could see the women reaching down into a box to pass out various gifts. I was excited . . . and then . . . she handed me . . . a book.

A book?

I looked at it, turned it over, and reread the title again: *The Bride Wears Combat Boots*[2]. What kind of a prize was this? What kind of a title was that? A picture of a white wedding dress, adorned with a beautiful bouquet of white star lilies and white roses, and a pair of black shiny combat boots prominently portrayed on the outside front cover. The subtitle stated, *Prepared for the Wedding – Prepared for the War! A Handbook of Spiritual Warfare.* Sounded kind of scary to me. I really couldn't take on any more wars right now.

I had no idea what this book might be about, nor did I care at that moment. I was so disappointed that I did not receive a pretty gift packet with cookies, candy, or aromatic soaps and lotions. I felt empty and betrayed once again. I believed that if I was beginning to be in God's favor, that

---

[2] *Lois A Hoshor: July I, 1998: Companion Press*

He would now let me have the desires of my heart. We went back to our room, and I threw the book into the top of my lockbox. I had no desire to read this paperback piece of literature. I pouted until I fell asleep.

Welcome Into This Place

Fortunate to have almost every Sunday evening off work in the kitchen, I attended church services with Sofie and Angel. I especially loved the opening song as we entered the congregation room and walked down the aisle to take our place among the other women:

> *Welcome into this place.*
> *Welcome into this broken vessel.*
> *You desire to abide in the praises of your people,*
> *so we lift our hands, and we lift our hearts*
> *as we offer up this praise unto your name.*[3]

And lift my hands in praise, I did. It was such a calming and reassuring hymn. I firmly believed and felt as though I were truly asking and welcoming the presence of the Lord into my heart.

The sermons and chapel time consisted of various churches, pastors, singing groups, or other Biblical spiritual teachers who would come and volunteer their time with us. Raised a Catholic, this Southern Baptist, Pentecostal, and/or other various Spirit-filled types of teachings, singing, dancing and praising God, was all new to me. Now I knew *for certain* that if my Mother could only see me now, she

---

[3] *Unknown*

would be absolutely mortified! I would sing, clap my hands, and raise my arms in honor and worship of God!

". . . and those the LORD has rescued will return. They will enter Zion with singing; everlasting joy will crown their heads. Gladness and joy will overtake them, and sorrow and sighing will flee away." Isaiah 35:10

More Good News

"Friend!" I heard Mr. Boyd's loud and booming voice soar up the open stairs and through the hallways. "Notice pick-up!"

I darted down the steps and responded, "Yes, sir? I have a notice?" He quickly handed me the much-anticipated memo that I was scheduled to sit for my college aptitude tests. Instructed to report to the Dean's Office to obtain study guides before the exam date, I was truly excited, albeit very anxious as I anticipated this upcoming opportunity to actually be able to attend college.

I immediately shifted over to Sofie's desk in the dorm library and let her know of my good news.

"I've never done anything like this Sofie. What if I don't do very good 'cause you know it's been years since I've been in school?"

Peering over the top of her reading glasses at me, she scolded, "Now what kind of talk is that for someone who believe in Jesus? You got this girl. You smart. Now quit worrying so much." In spite of her rebuke . . . she encouraged me.

I was also excited to share my good news with Miss C the following day at work. She was pleased and told me to study hard, explaining that I could certainly accomplish what I had determined to do! For the first time in a long time, I felt hope, promise and the possibility that my dream could now come true. *Thank you, Lord!* I thought to myself as I joyfully finished stirring the vegetable soup for lunch that day.

Within a few days, I also received notification that the date and time had been set for me to appear before the Parole Board regarding the possibility of release to a halfway house in June. I was to come prepared with my request and presentation of why I should be permitted to be released into this program. Enthralled with this news, I now worked exceptionally hard at both my studies and request for release. Perhaps one of the most important papers I would ever write, I knew I had to be thoughtful, professional and sincere in my request. I fervently prayed and asked God to help me with the exact wording regarding my sincere remorse, and the true desires of my heart for the future. I felt confident and hopeful with my finalized presentation.

Now the last week of the month, I was filled with hope and anticipation as I called home and excitedly shared my good news with Don. I knew he was struggling with this long separation of time.

"I promise you, honey. I will be home before you know it. Please just hang in there for me a little while longer. I know it's been really hard on you and everyone, but it won't be long now. I promise!" I said with emotion. I just knew that I knew that I would be coming home soon. I had been a model prisoner and worked hard at everything I was involved in. I was genuinely remorseful, and I knew that God heard my prayers.

"Well, we'll see. It just seems like so long ago that you left me, and now I'm not sure what to do," he said without emotion.

I was remarkably confused; he had emphatically stated that he was so sure that things were going to work out for us just a few weeks ago.

And I certainly didn't *choose* to leave him! But I knew it would all be over soon enough, and we would work everything out.

"Don, please understand that if you just have faith in God, all of this will work out and I'll be home soon."

"I told you before. Do not talk to me about God! The one and only thing I ever asked of Him was to save my son, to take me instead. I'm the one who didn't deserve to live. That boy never did anything in his life to deserve death, but God took him anyhow! He had everything to live for, his whole life ahead of him . . . and for what? So, no! Do not tell me about your God! I don't want to hear anymore!" I could hear the deep hopelessness in his quivering voice.

I always knew that Don was bitter and troubled beyond all understanding over the death of his youngest son. Todd was only 18 when he went off to college that September, and when he returned home for Thanksgiving break, it was obvious he was very ill. He never returned to college that fall and passed into eternity the following winter, taken by cancer. I could have never imagined in a million years what it would be like to lose one of my children. I could only believe that Don was going through this deep depression of loss and fear once again. I didn't know how to help him, but I wasn't deterred – I held onto hope for us. After all, I had enough faith for both of us now. I prayed and believed more than ever before.

"I'll call you at the end of the week. I have my hearing on Friday and I promise I'll have good news by then. And I have my college entrance exams tomorrow. I love you."

"Ok, I love you too. Good luck with everything," he awkwardly answered.

I walked slowly back upstairs to my cell. I had been so filled with hope - and yet the fear of denial and dashed dreams of freedom, acceptance into college, or my continued relationship with the man I loved so dearly, would not leave my head. *Oh, stop it! You have faith in God. Everything is going to be ok. Stop worrying and just keep moving ahead,* I boldly told myself. To bolster my confidence, and clear my head of any other negative thoughts, I stayed up late that night to finish studying for my exams, until I drifted off to sleep.

The Devastation of Dreams

I arose at 6:00 am the following morning. I wanted to get an early start of my chores before the day started, in order that I would have extra time to cram before my exam scheduled at 8:00 am. I was anxious, yet eager to start the tests. Except for math, which had always been my downfall, I felt fairly confident of the other subjects. I went over those algebra and statistics questions again and again.

Sofie brought me back a muffin for breakfast. "Thanks girlfriend! I appreciate it. I'm a nervous wreck."

"You'll be fine. You know you got this. Now get on

downstairs before you late," she scolded me, as usual. "And take you something to drink in there!"

I made my way downstairs, filled with apprehension, stopping at the water cooler to pour a cup of water and calm my nerves. As I entered the Dean's office along with about six other inmates, we were instructed to take our seats situated in the small classroom located directly across the hallway. Once we were seated, sharpened pencils were distributed, along with a 12-page booklet of questions. Upon instruction, we were to open our books and begin - then once completed, to drop them off across the hall in the Dean's office. We had one hour to finish. I guessed they would be able to tell if you were smart enough to get into college within that time frame.

I felt fairly good about my answers. I dropped off my test papers and headed back upstairs to my room to rest until 10:00 am count. Joy was on her bunk writing a letter when I entered the room.

"Hey Joy. What are you doing?"

"Writing to my Grandpa about the boys. Hope they're doing ok, and to see if he could send me 20 bucks. Where you been?"

"Just finished my college entrance exams. I think I did ok. I feel pretty good about it." I knew Joy was in college and seemed to be doing well with her studies.

"Did I hear you sayin' that you might be going to a halfway house in June?" she inquired.

"Well, I hope so. I have my hearing on Friday."

"You do understand that if you have any chance at all to get out of here for halfway house, the judge won't let you go if you in college?" she advised me.

"What do you mean? Why not?" I was worried to ask.

"Cause if you in anything that is a positive, learning program that will help you more on the outside, they not gonna let you leave here until you done with that. This is your only chance to get those programs, so they make you stay until you complete them."

"Who told you that? Are you sure?" I asked in disbelief.

"Look, you don't have to believe me, but you better check before you go signing up for anything. You have to decide if you want to go home or go to college."

"But you're going to school."

"Girl, I'm gonna be sitting here for at least another two years. I don't have a chance to get outta here early."

I couldn't possibly be hearing what she just told me. But I guess it made sense. This was the end of the month, and I could possibly be leaving here within another three or four months. I decided I would check with the Dean's office. Maybe I could just take one quarter of classes? But then what good would that do? I sure couldn't afford to continue with my classes once I was on the outside.

The following day I was called downstairs to speak with the Dean herself. As I was escorted into her office, she inquired "Friend?"

"Yes, ma'am."

"I wanted to talk to you personally because I wanted to let you know that you have one of the highest tests scores I have ever seen at this facility for entrance exams. You earned a 97% score."

She paused and looked me over. "And you did this *all on your own?*"

I was immediately taken aback. What did she mean?

"Yes ma'am. I did." I was angry now. I knew she was insinuating that I must have cheated.

"Well, then I guess we will see. You need to be in college. You have the ability to make great progress through our courses and we would like for you to sign up for the Spring quarter."

At that point, I wasn't sure I wanted to at all. I was so mad, and so hurt. But what should I have expected? After all, I had lied and cheated my way into this prison. If I was such an "intelligent" person, what was I doing in a place like this anyhow? Obviously, I had no common sense!

"I do have a question. If I should begin my classes, and then have the opportunity to go home early, will the judge not permit me to leave?"

"I can't speak for the judge, but I could most certainly see why a judge would be hesitant to pull you out of your classes. Yes, that could be a possibility. But this is such a good opportunity for you to be able to attend classes for free. You should seriously think about it. Get back with me in a few days if you should decide to register. Deadline is March 6th."

I left her office feeling very defeated and confused. I was elated that I did so well on my exams, and yet so wounded that my sin would indeed follow me throughout my life. I truly had to pray and think about what to do. I decided I would wait until I received my answer regarding the halfway house. Then I would know for sure what I should do.

"Guide me in your truth and teach me, for you are God my Savior, and my hope is in you all day long."   *Psalm 25:5*

Early Friday morning, I looked through my presentation once again, just to ensure I covered everything I wanted to say. Another day of butterflies, yet my hope in God dwelt deep within the pit of my stomach. There would be no time for breakfast this morning. I was afraid I couldn't hold anything down anyhow.

"Ok, I'm headed over to the parole hearing. Wish me luck!" I directed my words at both Sofie and Angel that morning.

"Good luck girlfriend! I hope you get to leave here soon enough," Angel declared with a bright attitude.

"Look. I really hope you get to go on the outside, but don't be disappointed if you don't," Sofie offered. "You know most people don't ever get to get out on they first hearing."

Once again, I felt confused. *Why would she say that to me?* I had been desperately praying and dreaming of being able to go home more than anything. I had so much hope and faith within my heart. I had been so good, and worked so hard, why wouldn't they consider letting me go to a transition house before being released? I only had another eight months to serve; it only made sense they would allow me to serve my few last months trying to get a job and shift back into society. I knew Sofie was only trying to "mother" me again, but I was feeling very confident. *She would see!*

I took my place along the long wooden benches in the hallways outside the hearing room, seated with at least another 20 women hoping to make their way home soon. I was situated near the end of the benches, so I really couldn't hear any kind of communication taking place on the other side of the doors. What I did see, was inmate after inmate coming back through the doors after their hearing, sobbing and heartbroken. I truly felt great empathy for them, knowing I couldn't bear it if I should be denied parole. But I was absolutely certain that would not be my demise.

At long last, my name was called, and I entered the room with confidence and assurance that my plea would sway even the toughest of hearts. I walked into a much smaller room than I had anticipated, not like a courtroom setting at all, except that the one lady and two gentlemen seated behind a long table were so formal and stringent in their character.

"Ms. Friend?" one of the gentlemen asked me.

"Yes sir."

He continued to list the crimes I had committed, the charges the state had brought against me, the names of my victims, the depth of the severity of these charges, and the appropriate punishment of such a crime. He then asked me why I should be considered to have the opportunity to attend a transition house, and not have to serve the remainder of my sentence within the prison.

Suppressing my fists together, and with a sick feeling in the pit of my stomach now, I humbly gave my dissertation of acceptance of guilt and responsibility: explaining the shame and outright disgrace, heartache and hardship I had caused for my victim, and so many other innocent people. I continued, stating that in a very foolish and senseless attempt to hold everything together, I had made horrible decisions to lie, steal and rob from my largest client. But now the time had come to face the ugly truth, to accept the responsibility for my own inexcusable actions. I could no longer go through life blaming everything corrupt or evil in my life on everyone else. I had made this deplorable decision all on my own. After spending several weeks of prison life feeling pitiful and sorry for myself, I had made up my mind "the buck stops here". I was a changed and determined woman of faith now.

Deep down, I was certain that even if they should scold me and tell what a horrible thing I had done; they would certainly understand the best option would be for me to have this opportunity to learn how to operate on the outside again.

One by one, each of the board members questioned me, admonished and reprimanded me in every way possible. I fully expected it. I fully deserved it. The last one to speak to me was the woman board member. I was certain that the softer side of a woman would scold me, but reluctantly see her way to the only logical solution.

Relieved to have finished presenting my case and eager for their verdict, I searched their faces for a hint of their decision and waited while they scribbled notations and whispered among themselves. Finally, they delivered their decision, and the flurry of heavy anticipation within my heart turned into complete mortification and devastation.

"Ms. Friend. I do *not* honestly believe that you sincerely understand the full extent of your crime, or the extreme consequences punishable by law for such an outlandish offence. Do you realize that this crime is punishable by law at the very minimum of three years, with a maximum sentence up to 25 years? I am appalled that you have already been granted such a lenient sentence of only one year. Therefore, NO, you will not be granted the opportunity to leave this prison. You are dismissed."

No. I knew she could not be done with her critique yet.

She was only telling me why I shouldn't be permitted to go home; but in a minute would say I needed to prove myself a better person, a better citizen, and would be granted the opportunity to do so. I sat there with a shocked look on my face and waited for her to tell me the correct answer.

But there was no other answer. That was the final decision.

I left the room in utter despair, tears running down my face, just like all the other women I had watched coming out of that room. I don't even remember walking back to the unit. I only remember lying on my bed and sobbing like a baby. I couldn't do this anymore. I couldn't make it for another eight months. Devastated, my heart and dreams shattered once again.

Why God, why? I don't understand! I've been trying so hard to believe in you and have faith . . . but there is no hope for me. I'm a horrible, wicked person. I don't deserve anything. Why would I ever think that I would? I hate myself. I hate living. I don't want to be here anymore!

The Final Break

I called home later that night, but Jennifer told me Don wasn't there. She told me then that he had been acting really strange lately and hadn't been coming home at night.

"What do you mean?" I was in more distress than ever.

"I don't know, Mom. He left me money on the table, but he hasn't come home at night the last two or three days. He left me a note and said he was visiting a friend." She hesitated but then went on, "I think he's getting ready to leave. I heard him talking to someone on the phone the other day and said he was thinking about leaving."

I thought I was going to throw up. I couldn't believe this was happening to me now, on top of everything else. My world was crashing down around me. What had happened to all of those promises, hope and belief I truly thought to be real? I held my head in disbelief and cradled the phone against my neck as I cried. I told Jennifer I wanted to come home to be with her right now. I wanted to hug her and tell her how much I loved her, and how sorry I was. But I also knew that I wanted someone to hold *me* and tell *me* they loved me.

"Don't tell Don I called. I will try to call him tomorrow during the day. I love you honey."

I hung up and immediately ran to my cell and went to bed. I turned on my side facing the white cement block wall and wept . . . and wished I wouldn't wake up . . . ever.

And then I didn't want to talk to God anymore. I didn't want to believe in Him anymore. All He did was to let me down and hurt me, over and over again, just like everyone else had done to me. I had tried so hard, but I was done with faith, hope and God. I was defeated.

Hezekiah turned his face to the wall and prayed to the LORD, "Remember, LORD, how I have walked before you faithfully and with wholehearted devotion and have done what is good in your eyes." And Hezekiah wept bitterly.   *2 Kings 20:2-3*

I tried several times the following day to reach Don. Jennifer told me he still hadn't come home. I wanted to call him at work but knew no one would accept a call from the

Women's State Prison. I could only ask Jen to leave a note for him to please be home on Sunday night so I could talk to him. It was very important that I speak with him.

I didn't go to church services Sunday evening. Sofie tried her hardest to console me and talk me into going, but I just couldn't. I was broken and shattered. I knew there wasn't going to be anything that would comfort or relieve me of the pain, confusion or grief.

I eventually mustered up enough strength to go down and make the dreaded phone call. When Don answered the phone, I tried to keep my composure. Deep inside I already suspected what he was going to say, I just tried desperately to believe it wouldn't be so. If he had taken time away to think things through, I was sure he would have come to the conclusion that he still loved me terribly.

"Hello. I've tried to reach you a few times, I began calmly, then blurted out, "Jennifer told me you've been visiting a friend. Who is that?"

After a long hesitation, Don answered. "Look dear. I really thought I loved you, but I just can't do this anymore." He broke down crying. "I have to leave now."

"Wait, what do you mean?" I insisted.

"I'm leaving. I have already paid everything up through March, but your daughter is going to have to be out by April 1st. She's going to have to go live with your parents." He paused. "I told you this wouldn't work. I can't do it."

"You can't do what? You can't live there anymore? Because of Jennifer? Because of me? What are you telling me? Are you leaving me?" I wouldn't allow myself to grasp what was happening. Although already somewhat suspicious, I could have never imagined that he would truly say these words to me.

"Nan, listen to me. Yes, I am leaving you. I am sorry, I really am. But I just can't stay here and know you're not coming home. Besides, everyone tells me that things will never change, that *you* will never change. It will only continue to get worse. I have to go."

"No wait!" I was afraid to ask. "Is there . . . is there someone else?"

I guess I already knew the answer. I knew that Don could not be without someone. "Yes, yes there is. There, now I've said it. Goodbye!" as he hung up the phone. I called again and again, but he wouldn't answer.

"What are you doing, you devastated one? Why dress yourself in scarlet and put on jewels of gold? Why highlight your eyes with makeup? You adorn yourself in vain. Your lovers despise you . ."   *Jeremiah 4:30*

CHAPTER 7

❧ *Clarification* ❧

transitive verb: to make understandable, clarify a subject; to free of confusion; to make clear or pure; to make or become more easily understood.

. . . And the glory of the LORD will be revealed, and all people will see it together. For the mouth of the LORD has spoken.   Isaiah 40:5

Truly devastated and beyond clarification of anything in my immediate existence, I had lost all sense of my very being on this earth. Severely depressed, I could barely manage to get out of bed each morning; only that it was required of me - without question. I recalled the young woman in boot camp at Maryswood who had been extremely ill, and the sergeant who mercilessly screamed at her, "Pick yourself up and count it out! Who told you, you could be sick on my watch? Did I give you permission to puke on my floor? Now start counting . . .!"

No one had given me permission to be depressed, hopeless or sick. *Why God? Why are you letting all these happen to me over and over again? I prayed, believed and trusted you!* I looked at God with anger, pain, distrust and confusion.

I soon became physically ill, with a cold, fever, coughing, sore throat and congestion. Sluggishly, I still attempted to participate in my aerobic classes (when you sign up for a class, you are expected to be there – I did not have permission otherwise); but I literally passed out during class and was taken by wheelchair to the infirmary located in my unit to see the nurse practitioner. I was diagnosed with a severe cold and ordered upstairs to my room where I was restricted to my cell, although fortunately provided with a 3-day pass from required classes and work. Someone would have to bring meals to me, but I really didn't feel like eating anything. I had requested Vicks VapoRub for my sore throat, cough drops, or cold medicine while at the medical unit, but never did receive anything other than Tylenol distributed by the nurse at each count. I was beyond miserable. Feeling sorely despondent, I just wanted to go to sleep and never wake up again. . . *ever*.

Sofie tried to comfort me but was very ill herself. It turned out she would soon be taken to the prison hospital across the street for gall bladder surgery. She was terrified to go to the infirmary as she had heard horror stories about that place, and I felt even more guilt as I wasn't very responsive to her needs. Sofie had helped me so much, and now when she needed me the most, I couldn't be there for her.

"Look ladies. Y'all need to eat some soup or something. Do you want some crackers, hot tea, or something else to drink?"

Angel and Joy tried to help both of us as much as they possibly could. Bless their hearts, they did indeed live up to their names, after all. But there was no amount of consoling, prayers, or hot liquids they could bestow upon us that would bring us out of our misery.

Sofie was transferred to the hospital for her surgery early

the following morning. Although I knew she was terrified to go, she was in so much pain and needed to be someplace where she could be taken care of. Joy and Angel asked if I needed anything, but they had to go to work, and I was left alone in my bunk. They said they would bring me something back for lunch.

I tossed and turned with anxiety and worry. I felt completely helpless and abandoned. *Please God … why have you left me? I don't feel your presence anymore. I feel alone and scared.*

I wanted to believe; I just wasn't sure I could anymore. I wanted to have faith, but now I was questioning my new-found belief, and feeling unworthy. I couldn't understand it. Had I not been faithful, read the Bible, and prayed every opportunity available to me? I had been excited about my recent understanding and hope of who God was. Blessed with so many miracles, I had been amazed at the answered prayers God had provided to me. He had made Himself known to me, and there was no doubt in my mind that He was real.

So why now, when I asked for the one thing I so desperately wanted, it was denied to me? I knew I could somehow survive not having the opportunity to go to college, or even the halfway house in June, but I truly couldn't bear that Don had left me. I recalled my previous prayer and plea with God to remove all of the bad things from my life. But I certainly didn't mean Don! How could he ever be bad for me? He was the one sure thing I had in my life. He was my rock, my protector, my one true love. I lay awake every night thinking about him being with someone else, and I just couldn't fathom the thought of it. My heart was shattered.

In addition, now Jennifer would have to leave and stay with my parents, and I would lose the apartment and the car Don had bought for me. How on earth would everything be moved out and put into storage? He just up and left me for someone else; and everyone else with all *my* responsibilities, problems, and worries. But maybe he was feeling the same about me; I had just up and left him with all the responsibilities too.

Now I had truly lost everything.

How long must I wrestle with my thoughts and day after day have sorrow in my heart? How long will my enemy triumph over me?
                                                                    Psalm 13:2

Something Good

Within a few days, I was finally permitted to call home to talk with my kids. I wanted more than anything else to see if there was any chance that Don had changed his mind and would stay? I tried to call the apartment, but no one answered. I called my oldest daughter Jodi at her house that night and learned that Jennifer was staying with her for the moment.

"No, Mom. He's moved all of his things out. But listen, all of us kids have talked, and we decided the best thing to do is to try to pay the rent and let Jennifer stay and finish out the school year."

"How on earth are you possibly going to be able to do that? And Jennifer can't stay by herself!" I asked in total disbelief.

"No, no. We talked with Don, and he said he was turning the child support checks over to us to pay the rent, and he would continue to pay the utilities for the next 2 months, but by June 1ˢᵗ, he's done. We're all going to take turns keeping Jen, or staying at the apartment with her, and getting her to school, work and cheerleading. We can do this for a few months. It'll be ok Mom."

How did I ever deserve such amazing kids? They had no idea the huge stress that was lifted from me at that moment. I could literally feel the weight of the tension and anxiety leave my body. This would at least buy me extra time to try to figure out other alternatives once June came. *Oh, why couldn't I have been released to the halfway house?*

"Does Grandma and Grandpa know?" I knew they would most likely want to step in and make Jennifer move back with them.

"I don't know if Don has said anything to them, but we haven't talked to them."

"Ok, please just leave it at that for the moment. But, if you can't do it anymore, make sure you ask for their help. Meanwhile, I'll try to figure something out about getting everything out of the apartment by June 1ˢᵗ." *And yet, what on earth did I possibly think I was going to be able to do? My release date was not until October 18ᵗʰ. I could do absolutely nothing!*

Later that same evening, I called Jill as she was going to be staying with Jen at the apartment that weekend. She let me know that Don had also said he would allow my son-in-law (her husband) to put my small red, 1984 two-door Ford Escape in Jason's name so that I could have a car when I came home. I could not thank her enough for doing these tremendous tasks for Jennifer and me. "Please, please thank

Jamie, Jason and everyone who is helping. I don't know how you're all going to do it, but thank you!"

This time when I hung up the phone, I was crying tears of great relief and gratitude for my kids and their spouses. I certainly didn't deserve it. For the first time ever, I realized how very much my children were thoughtful, caring and loving human beings, regardless of all they had suffered through while growing up. All I could think of was a verse in a song from *The Sound of Music*:

". . . So somewhere in my youth or childhood, I must have done something good. Nothing comes from nothing. Nothing ever could. So somewhere in my youth or childhood, I must have done something good."[4]

I was soon back to work in the kitchen, and although still miserable, at least it kept my mind off of things for several hours a day. I continued to call home and check in on Jennifer and my other children a few days a week. I was so homesick, and my heart ached for them.

I also missed Sofie terribly. Knowing she would be gone for several weeks, I wanted desperately to talk to her. Far worse than being trapped in this prison, I was trapped in anger and despondency. I was broken and couldn't seem to come out of this relentless state of sadness and misery. I stopped going to the church services on Sunday night, and I missed the date to sign up for the Spring quarter for college, but I didn't care. I had lost or thrown away everything I had

---

[4] *Somewhere in my Youth or Childhood: The Sound of Music; Richard Rodgers & Oscar Hammerstein II 1959*

finally come to believe in and hope for. . . and I had lost faith in God.

> *The LORD is close to the brokenhearted and saves those who are crushed in spirit.*   *Psalm 34:18*

The Sea of Galilee

Now well into the first weeks of March, I continued with my afternoon walks on the prison "walk-jog". I felt somewhat better when I could be outdoors and not locked up inside. The weather was becoming much warmer, and I could see and hear the birds chirping in the air. Oh, how I imagined that I could fly away with them up into the lingering clouds of the free and outside world. *Please, come and take me away with you!*

I continued to walk alone, still angry and confused, then softly within myself I cried out in deep desperation: *I don't understand, God; what do you want from me? Either take me from this world . . . or do something with me!*

Depressed to the point of suicidal thoughts, I reached out with immense hopelessness, yet just enough determination to not drown in my own sorrow. *You have to change me Lord because I don't know how!*

Shuffling along, I now picked up the pace so others wouldn't see the conspicuous tears running down my face.

Initially filled with constant fear and anxiety within the walls of the prison, I had become somewhat adjusted to the everyday life I was destined to spend for the remainder of my sentence. However, now I was more terrified than ever of what was to come next. Everything was falling down around me, and those I loved had deserted me. Neither Don nor my parents would talk to me. I was truly on my own now. With the exception of my children, how would I ever survive in the outside world after this? I was a thief, a cheat, and a liar. Who would ever trust me, let alone hire me? Who would ever believe or have confidence in me? Who would ever forgive me for the sins I had committed? I had lied to, stolen from and manipulated so many innocent people. I knew my life would never be the same again.

Don't you understand, God? I won't even be able to work at a gas station because I won't be trusted to handle other people's money. I'm going to lose what little bit I have left.

Now walking briskly on the warm black asphalt, feeling dreadfully sorry for myself, I gradually became aware of the image of "black ice" appearing before me. Believing the bright sun was reflective of the pavement, as well as the tears still clouding my eyes, I squinted at the continuous movement of the reflection on the path well ahead of me. However, I soon noticed a "rippling" effect of the illusion, giving me the sense that small waves of water were now surrounding me. I slowed my pace and then stopped abruptly. It appeared that with each step I took, the water was separating around the outline of my foot. Was I imagining this? I looked around to see if other walkers also noticed the "water" on the path. I wasn't usually afraid of water, but this was very strange, almost frightening.

And then, a whisper deep within my ear inquired of me *"Do you trust Me?"*

Okay, now I'm losing my mind for certain. I recalled only one other time that a voice, a thought, deep within my mind was speaking to me. That was also at a point in my life when I was so tormented and hopeless, I had attempted a very real suicide.

"Do you trust Me?" The thought penetrated even deeper. I knew then it could only be God.

"I don't know. I want to, but I'm afraid." I answered Him. Not wanting to give the impression to the yard security or others around me that I was oblivious to the physical world about me, I cautiously continued to walk forward, taking one slow step after another.

"Will you walk on the water with Me?"

I stopped abruptly, but then with each cautious step into "the water", I was well aware of the solid ground beneath me. I was instantly reminded of the story of Peter walking on the water with Jesus during the terrific storm:

. . . the boat was now in the middle of the sea, tossed by the waves, for the wind was contrary. Now in the fourth watch of the night Jesus went to them, walking on the sea. And when the disciples saw Him walking on the sea, they were troubled, saying, "It is a ghost!" And they cried out for fear. But immediately Jesus spoke to them, saying, "Be of good cheer! It is I; do not be afraid." And Peter answered Him and said, "Lord, if it is You, command me to come to You on the water." So He said, "Come." And when Peter had come down out of the boat, he walked on the water to go to Jesus. But when he saw that the wind was boisterous, he was afraid; and beginning to sink he cried out, saying, "Lord, save me!" And immediately Jesus stretched out His hand and caught him, and said to him, "O you of little faith, why did you doubt?" And when they got into the boat, the wind ceased."   *Matthew 14:24-32*

I knew what God was asking of me. He wanted me to turn my focus strictly on Him; to accept *Him* as my rock, my saving grace; to trust *Him* with all of my soul, and to ask Him even deeper into my heart. Only a few months before, I had fallen to my knees on the floor of my prison cell and had received Jesus into my heart. At the time I had been desperate and hopeless, filled with remorse and regret for all of the horrible things I had done. I had wanted Him to comfort me, love me, as well as to forgive and accept me, despite the sinner that I was. I had truly wanted to know who He was, and for Him to teach me all that He could. I had sincerely been seeking all of these things of Him.

But now He was seeking something of me. It was more than just God saving me from my lostness and horrific sins. It was more than Him telling me He had forgiven me and would always love me beyond measure. He had already done all of this by sacrificing His only Son for me. Now He wanted *me* to completely commit to *Him.* He wanted me to trust Him. He wanted me to follow His ways. I knew now that He wanted a relationship with me, and this was a two-way street, just as with any relationship with someone I loved.

I wasn't sure I could do that. That would mean giving up control of my life. I wasn't sure I knew how to be good enough to be in a committed relationship with God. That would mean no more going to the bars, drinking, partying, or sleeping with my boyfriend . . . or anyone other than a husband. I didn't know if I could give up this *control . . .* but then immediately succumbed to the brutal fact that *I wasn't in control of my life anyhow.*

I don't know God. I want to trust you, but I'm afraid

you'll let me down. Memories of the abuse I had endured since the time I was a young girl were revived in my mind. I had trusted and loved my father, previous marriages, relationships, and other men in my life . . . but they had all betrayed me in some form or another. I had been beaten, lied to, cheated on and stolen from. The people I thought loved me the most threatened, shot at, spit on, stalked and seduced me. Thoughts of fear for my life had been imbedded deeply into my soul. I was painfully afraid to ever let my guard down. How could I ever trust anyone again?

Okay, God, but please don't let me down or leave me. I can't take anymore. If I do this thing that you ask of me, please hold onto my hand. I'm not strong enough yet. Don't let go of me, Jesus. If you let go, I will never believe or trust anyone again. Hold on really tight.

I felt like a little girl again, holding onto the hand of my grandfather when he used to walk beside me. Papa was six feet tall and had very long legs . . . until he lost both of his legs due to severe infection. I was only three or four years old, but well remember running alongside of him, trying to stay up with his quick and long stride. Until the very day he passed from this earth, I had always cherished Papa with the innocence and faith only a child can have.

I gained more confidence with each step now. I imagined I was truly walking on the Sea of Galilee, walking into the arms of Jesus. I knew I had to keep my eyes on Him, straight ahead of me, or I would begin to sink. The heavenly, water-walking vision had given me instant relief of my fears. I wanted to tread lightly and carefully, yet gain confidence and reassurance that Jesus would be there for me.

Okay God, I'm ready now. I don't know how to do this, but I will trust you.

Do you not know? Have you not heard? The LORD is the everlasting God, the Creator of the ends of the earth. He will not grow tired or weary, and his understanding no one can fathom.   *Isaiah 40:28*

A Conversation with God

Then he said to them all: "Whoever wants to be my disciple must deny themselves and take up their cross daily and follow me. For whoever wants to save their life will lose it, but whoever loses their life for me will save it."   *Luke 9:23-24*

I continued walking, slowing, wanting to hold on to this moment of deep conversation with God.

What do you want me to do? How do I do this thing that you ask of me? Where do I go from here?

His words came softly…

Someday you will guide teenagers, write your story, and speak before thousands.

Now I knew I must have certainly misunderstood that message! As a single mom, I had just finished raising my four teenagers. I loved my children immensely but had no desire whatsoever to work with teenagers. And I strongly doubted that I should ever write, speak or teach others about anything at all.

But who am I, Lord? I am a liar and a thief. I am the lowest of all. Who would ever believe me? What would I ever have to say to them?

The message continued: *They will know because you know.*

Not at all convinced I would ever be worthy or knowledgeable enough of anything again, I instantly understood what He meant by that. I was brought back to the memory of watching a television broadcast of Joyce Meyer, an admired and well-liked Christian evangelist. Prior to my conviction, and in my earlier relentless and desperate search for answers, I had occasionally tuned in to watch this woman of God. Not really sure that I even liked her (due to her deep, raspy and boisterous voice), let alone understand many of her stories, Bible verses and teachings, I was finally fed up one day. I didn't know who the *Israelites* were that she kept referring to, or this mountain she was talking about that they kept walking around . . . for 40 years no less! What kind of God would tell His people to do that?

Eventually, I shouted at the television set, "Look lady, you have no idea what I have been through in my life. You have your perfect Christian family and your perfect Christian husband, your perfect hair and your perfect clothes. Until you have walked in my shoes, *DON'T* tell me about your God because He doesn't exist for me!"

At that moment, I jumped up to turn the channel on my old 1980-something console television, Ms. Meyer immediately began telling of her abusive father, her pregnancy at an early age, and the neglect of her first husband, and how she had been forced to humble herself and call her family to beg for bus fare so she could travel across the country to return home.

She then went on to explain how she met her current

and very *Christian* husband while washing her Volkswagen Beetle in her driveway one day, wearing only a bikini and drinking a beer. (That part of her story completely caught me of guard, to say the least!) I knew that Joyce had four children, and I also had four children. . . and as she continued with many other accounts and episodes of her life, I knew now she was telling *my story*. This I could understand! I slowly went back to my seat on the couch to listen. I wanted to know how God had brought her through these tragedies in *her* life.

Walking on the walk-jog "water", and reflecting on that message, I suddenly understood that people going through fear, pain and suffering would believe me because they would know I had walked in their shoes. God wanted me to tell them that He was very real today, just as He has always been from the beginning of time. He wanted me to tell people to have hope and have faith in Him again. He wanted me to share with them *my story*, because indeed, everyone has a story, a testimony, a painful experience in their life, and they could possibly relate to mine.

Okay, God. I understand, but I have an awful lot to learn. I will take this journey with you, but again, please don't let go of me. I need you now more than ever.

"For I know the plans I have for you," declares the LORD, *"plans to prosper you and not to harm you, plans to give you hope and a future. Then you will call on me and come and pray to me, and I will listen to you. You will seek me and find me when you seek me with all your heart. I will be found by you," declares the* LORD, *"and will bring you back from captivity. I*

will gather you from all the nations and places where I have banished you," declares the LORD, "and will bring you back to the place from which I carried you into exile."

Jeremiah 29:11-14

CHAPTER 8

❧ *Liberation* ❧

n. The act of liberation; the state of being liberated; the act or process of freeing someone or something from another's control: the act of setting free; emancipation, deliverance.

"You will not have to fight this battle. Take up your positions, stand firm and see the deliverance the LORD will give you . . . Do not be afraid; do not be discouraged. Go out to face them tomorrow, and the LORD will be with you always."
2 Chronicles 20:17

Saving Grace

Certainly, it must be time for Sophie to return to our dorm. It had been over three weeks now and I was truly worried about her. I had prayed that God would heal her, strengthen her, and give her great comfort. Where could she be?

Still lying-in bed that early April morning, I hung my head over the side of my top bunk - as if to verify that maybe I had only imagined Sophie had not returned yet, and that in reality she was right below me in her own bed.

"Why is it taking so long for Sofie to come back! She was terrified to go over there, and now we can't even get any word about how she is doing, or *IF* she is coming back," I worried aloud to my cell mates.

"Yeah, I know," Angel answered grimly. "I hear tell that place ain't no joke." She shook her head disapprovingly as she finished making her bed. "Mmm-mmm-mmm! One thing for sure, you can't get sick up in this place. Nothing good gonna come of it!"

"Nah, she'll be okay," Joy countered. "Just takes time to heal. She gotta be able to come back and go to work and everything. They not gonna let her just lay up in her bunk. You'll see. Quit worryin' so much!"

Reluctantly, I agreed. "And don't forget you got cleaning today," she reminded me as she quickly pulled her long dirty-blond hair up into a ponytail, gathered up her books and hurried off to breakfast and her Thursday morning classes.

Angel had finally been granted the opportunity she had hoped for: to go out into the community and work in the warehouse. I was pleased for her. She had to be ready and downstairs to leave by 7:15 am.

It was my day off work, and I was eager to go outside on the walk-jog and enjoy the Spring day, although first I desired to be lazy just a bit longer. Eventually I rolled out of bed, dressed, completed my cleaning chores, and then gathered paper and pens to take outside with me. It was supposed to be a little warmer this particular day - enough that I could sit outside on the picnic tables or bleachers at the basketball ball court/walk-jog and answer the letters and thoughtful cards I had received from a few good friends and my children.

My heart was especially softened by the crayon images

of the sun, flowers, green grass and stick figures of myself and grandsons they had so artistically exhibited upon bright colored construction paper. Their names prominently displayed in large "child script" block letters across the top of each drawing, I felt especially hopeful as they had precariously drawn such big smiles on our faces. Oh, the pure innocence of a child. It was refreshing and uplifting to know their young minds and hearts did not comprehend the evils of the world.

"And he said: "Truly I tell you, unless you change and become like little children, you will never enter the kingdom of heaven."   *Matthew18:3*

I had also received a request from my attorney to write and offer advice and encouragement to one of her clients from my hometown who had recently been sentenced to four years in Maryswood for embezzlement. This imprisoned woman never did respond to my letter of reassurance and support, but that was understandable. Sometimes it's too hard to even talk about your situation to others. It might take her some time of healing or acceptance, as it did for me.

Regardless, I was puzzled why she would receive such a harsh sentence when I had only been sentenced to one year. Of course, I didn't ask her that; but would (much) later learn she did not feel she had committed this crime; that she believed she was entitled to the money she had taken unlawfully, and felt no remorse whatsoever. I well-remembered this particular woman coming into the bank several times a week when I had worked there many years prior; bringing along her sweet three-year-old daughter. I could only think of that little girl with blond pigtails and blue eyes who would now be without her Mama for four long years. I was heart-broken for her.

I pulled on my dark navy-blue zip-up hoodie and headed outside into the fresh morning air, where the sun soothingly warmed my face, and lifted my spirits. I was beginning to feel some self-worth again. I had resumed my exercises of aerobics and walking, and had lost almost 30 pounds from the time I first entered Maryswood six months prior in October. My energy level was gradually being restored - but well beyond the physical improvements, the healing message that God had given to me just weeks earlier still filled my heart with encouragement and hope. I had never experienced that saving grace and inner feeling of self-worth and confidence as I did now. I knew that not only my physical health, but my mental and spiritual health were on the mend as well. I was getting stronger with each new day.

But he said to me, "My grace is sufficient for you, for my power is made perfect in weakness." Therefore, I will boast all the more gladly about my weaknesses, so that Christ's power may dwell in me.   *2 Corinthians 12:9*

I couldn't stop thinking of Sophie, however. *Please God, bring Sophie home to us soon. I just want to know that she is ok.* I now realized how much I truly missed my friend, my confidant, my *worldly* saving grace. And I wanted so much to be able to share with her the things God had revealed to me, and the message He had so graciously granted me. I knew that Sophie was the one person that would believe and understand exactly what had transpired on the walk-jog just a few weeks beforehand.

One night the Lord spoke to Paul in a vision: "Do not be afraid; keep on speaking, do not be silent."   Acts 18:9

The Ministry of Women

And we know that in all things God works for the good of those who love him, who have been called according to his purpose.   Romans 8:28

Once I completed my daily routine of walking; usually 6 to 8 laps around the basketball court/track - I eagerly headed over to the picnic tables to begin writing my letters. Subtly adding words of encouragement and loving notes about Jesus within each letter, I sealed up envelopes with words of His promise and hope for each of us. Within the final envelope addressed to my attorney Katherine, I not only enclosed the letter she had requested of me for the inmate, but a separate letter addressed specifically to her attention of which I inquired if she thought there might be any possibility I could apply for an early-judicial release?

I remembered Angel telling me when I first arrived at the Pre-Release Center, that after six months' time, anyone could apply for early release. I certainly was not convinced however, that I could possibly qualify as I had received a *mandatory* sentence of one year – and knew full well that this crime most often carried a minimum sentence of three years; but I also reasoned it couldn't hurt to ask. I heaved a huge sigh of *unbelief*, knowing full well this would most likely be yet another profound disappointment. But I also knew I would be okay with a denial this time. I truly wasn't expecting to be released, and I sincerely understood and believed that God had a plan for my life. I knew that whatever course God had chosen for me, it would be what He deemed best for me. I knew it would be what was pure, what was true, and what was right for *me*.

"Finally, brothers and sisters, whatever is true, whatever is noble, whatever is right, whatever is pure, whatever is lovely, whatever is admirable; if anything is excellent or praiseworthy, think about such things."   *Phil 4:8*

". . . so that you may be able to discern what is best and may be pure and blameless for the day of Christ."   *Phil 1:10*

As I sealed up the last envelope and gathered my belongings, I noticed an inmate sitting on the bleachers and softly crying. She looked up, then slowly approached me at the table and said she noticed I had been writing letters.

"Uhm. Do you think you could write a letter to my husband for me?" she asked with hesitancy. "I really can't write very well, and I'm not good with words. I don't even know what to say to him right now."

This meager woman was marked with a strikingly pale and scarred face, bad teeth and thinning, dull-brownish hair. Probably in her 30's or early 40's, she was dreadfully thin and sickly. She smoked a cigarette as she continued her story, drawing out each breath as if it might be her last.

She explained that her husband had given her numerous opportunities to get help and stop using drugs and alcohol. They had four children together, and this was the third time she had been imprisoned within the state facilities, not to mention all the county jail time she had served. "Please tell him I love him, and I know he doesn't believe me, but I really am sorry. I just want to go home and be with my family," she sniffled.

My heart softened for her, and yet I couldn't help but wonder what on earth had she not figured out the first three times she had been sentenced to prison, or all the times she had spent in the county jails? Certainly, there were programs she could attend, or classes she could go to that would help her?

But I also knew I couldn't even begin to imagine what it must be like to have such a powerful addiction controlling her every thought, decision and life choices. She unquestionably had a serious dependence that restrained her life in every way. What was *my* excuse for possessing such senseless and foolish thinking? I was sitting in prison right next to this woman with no other person or situation to blame except myself.

"Do not judge, or you too will be judged. For in the same way you judge others, you will be judged, and with the measure you use, it will be measured to you. Why do you look at the speck of sawdust in your brother's eye and pay no attention to the plank in your own eye? How can you say to your brother, 'Let me take the speck out of your eye,' when all the time there is a plank in your own eye? You hypocrite, first take the plank out of your own eye, and then you will see clearly to remove the speck from your brother's eye." Matthew 7:1-5

My heart truly ached for her. I knew I could only do what God asked of me to do for this woman – to write this letter for her, and to encourage her the only way I knew how.

Surprisingly, I began to share my story with her and to tell her of all the things God had done for me just within the time that I had been imprisoned. I told her that nothing is impossible for God. And then quite surprised at myself again, I asked her if I could pray for her? I just kept thinking that is what Sofie would do.

"Oh, yes. Would you please?" she began to gently weep again.

Oh great. Somehow, I was hoping she would say *no*. I really didn't know what to say, or how to pray. I tried to think about what Sofie would say to her. I stumbled through a prayer, but as I continued to speak, the words just seemed to come to me. And I remembered what Sofie had taught me to say at the end of each prayer - ". . . in Jesus' name. Amen." (Our prayers to the Father must come through Jesus, who took away the separation between us and God.)

Jesus answered, "I am the way and the truth and the life. No one comes to the Father except through me."   *John 14:6*

Although I didn't realize it at the time, I would later understand that on this day, God had shown His purpose for me to begin my ministry to women. I would eventually come to understand that ministry to others is often just listening to people's pain and suffering; offering a kind word of understanding and empathy; possibly to write a letter to them, or *for* them; but always to offer prayer, hope and love when they have no one else to do that for them.

I would also come to realize that ministering to others helped me to heal, and shed light about my own life experiences, as well: the sins and the loss of my business, my family, my boyfriend, my pride and dignity; the sense of who I was, as well as the root of these problems. Continued searching and reading the Word of God (Bible) also helped me to understand the fruit of the blessings and promises God had in store for me; for all of His children who would truly seek Him.

"Create in me a pure heart, O God, and renew a steadfast spirit within me."   *Psalm 51:10*

On the walk-jog that day almost a month earlier, I had asked God to please take away everything and everyone that was bad in my life; to make me be pure again. *Not* at all that Don was a bad person; it was that the relationship and circumstances were bad for *me.* He had always been very good and loving to me, but I knew that I *knew* that if I had gone back home to him, I would soon begin to run the bars, resume drinking and sleeping with him again. I could not go back to that way of life anymore. I did not want to go backward in my journey with God. I also found myself incredibly surprised at how much God had changed my mindset and my heart. I knew then that once I had *genuinely* accepted and asked Jesus to come into my heart, to change me, to cause for me to be a better person . . . He did just that. The true Spirit of God now lived within me - because I had sincerely invited Him in.

Ask and it will be given to you; seek and you will find; knock and the door will be opened to you. For everyone who asks receives; the one who seeks finds; and to the one who knocks, the door will be opened.   *Matthew 7:7-8*

Cooking up a Storm

One of four cooks in the kitchen cooking for over 500 women and staff over the past three months now, I would often add spices/butter/flavorings, or possibly changing up the menu items for the day; with permission of Mr. Y, of course. The dinner menu that night was to be cold lunchmeat & cheese sandwiches with Wonton Soup. Someone forgot to unpack the frozen lunchmeat that morning, so I offered to make grilled cheese sandwiches for everyone. Mr. Y cautioned it would be very difficult to make over 500 hot sandwiches, but if I wanted to do it, go for it.

"Hey Friend. Good looking out!" some of the ladies shouted over the counters as I stood over the huge griddles quickly buttering and flipping as many sandwiches as I possibly could. Mr. Y eventually stepped in and worked alongside me at the grill.

At the end of each lunch/dinner shift, while others cleaned and scrubbed pans and the floors, it was now my responsibility to pack up covered dishes to be distributed to the inmates in the "hole". I pushed the cart piled high with trays of food and drink and would accompany the CO throughout the grounds and down long dark hallways of the lock-down facility. As we approached each bolted door with a small 8" x 8" window, the CO would loudly announce that it was mealtime and order the inmate to step back as the "mail-slot" door was opened. I would then slide the meal plate through the opening as instructed. Most would be thankful, but there were always those who would yell and curse at us "'bout time they be gettin' some food up in here!", sometimes order the food to be taken away, or not acknowledge us at all. I began to silently pray for each of these women.

"About midnight Paul and Silas were praying and singing hymns to God, and the other prisoners were listening to them."
Acts 16:25

Bad News Bowman

"Friend! What you doin' saying I'm a liar!" Joy charged into the cell one day.

"What are you talkin' about? I didn't say that! Who told you that?" I shot right back.

"Bowman over at the kitchen said you been talkin' 'bout me and said I was a liar!"

I immediately knew who she was talking about. "Bowman" was a large, strong, and offensive dark-skinned black woman who seemed to pretty much hate the world. She was always stirring up trouble for everyone, complained about everything, never cleaned or worked hard at anything, and was clearly miserable with herself. Most of the time I just steered clear of her, but one day Mr. Johnson asked where she was, and then told me to go in the back to see if she was in the restroom. Reluctantly, I walked down the long hallway to the restroom/storage area. I really wasn't crazy about being back there by myself with her.

"Bowman? You in there? Johnson lookin' for you!" I loudly spoke through the bathroom door.

"Friend? You better just walk away if you know what's good for you!" she screamed back at me. I could hear more than one voice whispering in the bathroom. I immediately turned around and left without saying a word.

"Where Bowman at?" Mr. Johnson inquired. I only nodded toward the hallway. "Ok, I got it," he replied as he let out a sigh.

"You shouldn't be snitchin' on people Friend," Deidra quietly cautioned me as she placed chocolate-chip cookie dough on the extra-large cookie sheets. Deidra was an older white woman in her late 40's or possibly 50's; thick dark black hair with white streaks throughout rolled up in a bun on top of her head, accentuating her harsh, wrinkled facial features, heavy black eyeliner and mascara caked on her eyelashes. Although currently serving time for running a house of prostitution and drugs, she was most usually easy to get along with. She appeared to have had a pretty rough life and was offering up what she deemed to be sound advice. "You don't know what that girl is capable of," she whispered.

"I didn't say a word. He already knew she was back there. Probably just doesn't know Bowman is not the only one in that bathroom," I quietly replied.

"Yeah, but she ain't gonna see it that way. Just watch your back," once again offering her worldly and expertise advice.

"Ok, I hear you. Thanks." I went back to preparing the melted butter with garlic salt to be brushed on giant loaves of bread that night for dinner. I tried to stay focused on my work and just ignore Bowman and her "companion" as Mr. Johnson escorted them into the office to be written up. She glared at me as she passed by, but I just kept stirring that butter and garlic with great determination and vigor. I didn't want to acknowledge her at all. I couldn't take another "Peaches" episode like I did at Maryswood. (Refer to Volume 1- ***Defining Truth***. Story of inmate sentenced to life for murder - who had "put the word out" on me.) I had felt safe at this facility and didn't want that to change now.

It would be several days later that Bowman approached me in the kitchen, gradually leaned over the work-table directly across from me with her arms crossed and quietly announce, "So your roomie said you always being a snitch on everyone. Said you lie just to be a "f …ing" bi…! You think you something special up in here or somethin' Friend?"

"That's not true! Who told you that? I know that none of my roomies would say that!" I retorted back at her. I wasn't necessarily being quiet, so Bowman bolted upright and looked around to see who might be in the area.

The she leaned back in and whispered boldly, "Oh, so now you sayin' *they* lyin' too? Humm . . . We'll see 'bout that!" as she grinned like an evil witch with attitude and walked away. "Oh yeah. . . we see about that!"

Now as I spoke with Joy, I understood what had happened. "Look Joy I never said that about you or anyone! She just tryin' to start a fight between us 'cause she thinks I called her out to Mr. Johnson in CFS. That's what this is all about." I continued to explain to her what had happened and that now Bowman had it out for me.

"So, you never said that I was a liar and a snitch?" she angrily glared at me.

"No! I swear to you! Please don't believe her. I would never say that about you!" I insisted. *Oh, dear God. Please, please stop the insanity!*

I continually looked over my shoulder after that. The feeling of fear and dread returned to my heart. I knew deep down this was Satan working overtime to take me down.

But I stayed diligent with my prayers for protection and peace.

"But let all who take refuge in You be glad; let them ever sing for joy. Spread your protection over them, that those who love your name may rejoice in you."   *Psalm 5:11*

April Showers Bring . . .

Thursday morning, my day off, and it was pouring down torrential rains outside. I was definitely going to lay in bed for as long as I possibly could this morning. I pulled the covers up around my neck, turned toward the wall and closed my eyes for a few minutes.

"What you think you doing still in bed Friend?"

Oh, my goodness, I knew that familiar and long-lost voice! I quickly jumped up and off the bed. "Sofie! Oh my gosh, where have you been? I have missed you so much girl!" I squealed with delight and pure joy as I ran to hug her wet and cold body.

"You know I been over at the hospital. But I sure missed all of you too! That ain't no joke over there for real," as she continued to tell me of all the pain, surgery, recovery, her "drama" roommate at the hospital; and all the mischief she somehow managed to escape when she tried to sneak out and use a phone and get some water. She had been through a lot, and I wanted to hear everything she had to say.

"Sofie, I want to know everything about what happened, and I have so much to tell you too, but first I have to run downstairs and get the cleaning stuff to get this room cleaned before count. I'm off today, so we'll have time. I'll be right back. Can I get you anything while I'm down there?" I asked excitedly. I was just so relieved and pleased to see my friend again.

After count that morning, Sofie and I hung out in our room, went to lunch, and spent several hours catching up on all the news, gossip and everything going on at the compound within the past month. I told her about Bowman and Joy; that Angel got her new job outside the grounds, and the new inmate that was located right next door to us who was serving time for murder – of her own four-year old daughter.

"I sure don't understand why she's serving time here. She said her boyfriend did it, but she stood by and didn't turn him in right away. I don't know, maybe she was given a lesser charge. Anyhow she's pregnant right now, and everyone keeps calling her a baby killer and sayin' she doesn't deserve to have this baby. She is afraid and wants to be moved, but they already moved her here from up north. She needs protection for sure."

Even though I couldn't imagine in my wildest dreams what she could have possibly been thinking (again, not my place to judge *anyone*), I still didn't want to see anything bad happen to her or the baby she was carrying. She needed to be able to have the baby safely, the child taken from her, and then she should serve her time justly.

Regardless, more than anything else, I was especially excited to be able to share with Sofie my experience on the walk-jog and the very words that God had spoken to me. I told her about the woman who wanted me to write a letter for her and how I prayed with her. "I just thought about what I knew you would do Sofie. I remembered what you told me about praying in the name of Jesus. I just wanted to help her."

"You did right, girlfriend. That's good! I know that God has big plans for you someday. But just keep listening to Him. Remember to pray for discernment so you'll always know the truth and the difference between what is from God, and what the lies from Satan are. Remember that God will never lie to you, or instruct you of anything that is bad or evil for you to do. Just keep praying for truth."

"Ok, thank you," as I shook my head in agreement.

"I am your servant; give me discernment that I may understand your statutes."   *Psalm 119:125*

. . . New Freedom . . .

Later that afternoon as we continued to talk, laugh, and eat cheese crackers in the game room, the CO on duty hollered for me to come to her desk. Bolting over to the circular desk, I inquired, "Yes ma'am?"

"You need to report to the Sergeant's office in Unit 5. You can sign out and go over now."

I had never been called in by any of the officers before. I couldn't imagine what this might be regarding. I told Sofie I'd be back, and we would talk more later.

As I grudgingly made my way to Unit 5, I earnestly searched my mind. *What might I have done wrong?* Just like when you're a kid and get called to the principal's office, I prepared for the worst. I could only hope that I was not to receive a *ticket* for something I might have done. (A *ticket* is a written reprimand that goes against your record. Often when an inmate is required to report to the Sergeant's office, it is to receive a ticket. Too many tickets and you could go to the hole.) My only thought was of something that possibly Bowman was trying to get me mixed up into some sort of turmoil. Regardless, I entered the unit and indicated that I was to report to the Sergeant's office.

"Friend? Have a seat and Sergeant Collins will be with you in a minute," the inmate at the front desk instructed.

I recognized this woman from my Theft class (serving time for insurance fraud) and church services. Miss Lillian was an older, lightly complected black woman with dark blemishes, short graying wiry hair, large protruding teeth, and wore *those 80's* thick lens, octagon rim glasses. I remembered her so well because I always thought she looked and sounded like the *Honey Bunches of Oats* woman in the TV commercial. I had to wonder if the cereal lady had indeed committed a crime.

A few minutes later a petite, white woman with perfectly white teeth, a smooth and rosy complexion, short blond hair, and blue eyes appeared from the hallway. "Friend? Come on back." I immediately followed her down the hall and into a small office.

"I'm sure you are wondering why you have been called over to see me?" as she rounded her desk to be seated.

"Yes ma'am." I quietly answered.

"Well, I understand that you might be going home soon? Is that correct?" as she proceeded to look through some papers.

Puzzled, I replied "No, Ma'am. Not that I know of." I was completely caught off guard by this question, but certainly hoping there might be some truth to it!

"But that's what you have been telling your family, isn't it?" she continued.

I knew immediately she was referring to the things I had said and promised to Don just a few months earlier about going to the halfway house. I also knew right then that someone had been listening in on my calls (as they often do) and heard me tell Don of this possibility in my attempt to try to hold everything together. I had also told my children the same thing: more so of what I had *hoped* and wanted to *believe* would take place.

"No ma'am. That's not going to happen now. I was hoping that would be a possibility at the time, but the parole board didn't approve my request. I understand now that I need to stay here and finish my time."

Regardless, it made me wonder *what else I might have ever said that now I might be in trouble for?* I couldn't think of anything. I also knew the staff always went through the mail when it came in to make sure there was no contraband, inappropriate pictures, conspiracy situations (to escape, etc.). But I honestly could not think of anything at all that I might have said or written at any time that would cause me to be in any kind of trouble.

She then asked me if my fiancé would be waiting for me when I returned home? I explained that Don was not my fiancé and was no longer my boyfriend either.

"Oh, because funny that somehow everyone in here now has a fiancé or a husband, even though they're not married or promised to be."

I didn't understand at all what she was asking me or trying to get at. I felt as though she only wanted to dishearten me, and that she was aware of anything and everything I had ever said or done within the facility. I was not impressed at all by her obvious intimidation, and just wanted to leave.

"Regardless, I called you in here because I understand that you can type and have experience with office work? Is that correct?"

"Yes ma'am. I do," wondering how she would know that.

"There is an opening at the event center (located within the warehouse) for office work if you are interested. It pays a little more, you will only work Monday through Friday from 8:00 am - 4:00 pm and have every weekend off. Please understand that you will be working outside of this facility, and we must know that we can trust you."

I now realized why she was questioning me: to see if I would be truthful. She explained that she had done her background check into my history of behavior, goals, classes I had attended; if I would be considered "high risk", and/ or if I would be leaving the facility anytime soon. I had successfully completed all of my alternative classes, would not be attending college classes nor going home soon - and according to my conversations and correspondence, was not considered high risk. Therefore, I was approved to go outside of the prison on a daily basis. I breathed a huge sigh of relief to myself, and deep inside I was shouting out *"Thank you God! Thank you!"*

After more instruction, discussion, and paperwork, I thanked Sergeant Collins for this opportunity and couldn't wait to go back to tell Sofie of my good news!

When I returned, Sofie was in her bunk trying to rest. She turned over to face me as we picked right back up with our conversation, now adding this remarkable report of God's blessing. I was excited to tell her I would now be making almost $1.00 per hour, and I was going to help her to get some of the things she wanted. Like a new pair of tennis shoes that she desperately needed!

We were so busy talking and laughing, that we lost track of the time. It was now close to 4:00 pm count time, and a new CO, Miss Jones, was on duty. Sofie and I were both still on our bunks conversing and giggling when she came into the room and stood at the doorsill. Our cell was the very first door at the top of the stairs and count always started with us.

A young, thin and attractive black woman with jet black hair pulled up firmly in a bun - Miss Jones had the temperament and manner of a commanding officer that demanded respect and a "no excuses" attitude. She would not tolerate insubordination, poor justification or excuses of any kind.

"What are you doing? It's count time!" she screamed at us with hands on her hips. "You *know* you are to be on the floor, at attention, facing straight ahead and NO talking or laughing! Both of you report to me downstairs as soon as count is over! Do you understand?"

We both answered simultaneously as we hurriedly scrambled to our standing position on the floor, "Yes ma'am!"

Then in an awkward attempt to explain why we were not at attention when she entered the room, Sofie blurted out "We are sorry, but Mr. Boyd and the other COs always announce that it's count time and then we get ready. We didn't hear you."

"What? Announce count time? Why should I have to announce count time? You know it's 4:00 o'clock every day. Am I correct?"

"Yes ma'am," Sofie answered. "But we didn't realize what time it was."

"That's not my problem! It's your responsibility to know when it's time for count! You have a watch, don't you?" as she glared at the watch located on my wrist.

"Yes ma'am," I sheepishly answered.

"Ok, then you have no excuse and I expect both of you at my desk immediately after count!" as she walked out of the room.

Sofie and I both looked at each other with fear and anxiety as we knew we could get a ticket for sure. I almost started crying, having received news only an hour earlier that I would be able to work outside the grounds, and now I was facing a ticket that might prevent me from going out.

Almost immediately we could both hear Miss Jones yelling at the other inmates the same exact thing - that they *know* it's 4:00 pm count time! We could hear the ladies also try to explain that count time has always been announced prior to inspection, but to no avail. However, we did not hear the CO tell any of the other women they had to report to her desk. We held hands and quietly prayed this might influence the CO enough that we could possibly be spared charges of insubordination.

Immediately after count, Sofie and I made our way to the CO's desk and continued to be harshly scolded for our seemingly inability and immaturity to be aware of count time on our own, and that she should write us up and issue us a ticket. She asked if we could think of any reason why she shouldn't write us up? We both hung our heads and tears rolled down my face. This would be my first ticket ever, and

I just couldn't lose my chance to work outside. "No ma'am," we both softly answered.

"Why are you crying? There's no crying in here! You both need to grow up and face your responsibilities! Be responsible when you do something. Don't make excuses when you do something wrong! Can't you see I'm trying to help you? Now go to dinner and don't let me catch you out of place anymore! Do I make myself clear?"

Sofie and I both looked at each other out of disbelief, thanked Miss Jones (and God!), and then hurriedly made our way outside of the unit to go to CFS for dinner before she changed her mind.

Once outside, we agreed that most certainly Miss Jones was a young corporal *wanna-be*! "She straight up from the military for sure! She must a' been a staff sergeant!" Sofie confirmed my very thoughts.

"Do not be afraid of them; the LORD your God himself will fight for you."   *Deuteronomy 3:22*

When we returned to the dorm, we all stayed in our room that night. We could hear Miss Jones scolding several other women about being in the laundry room, having the TV turned up too loud, and making too much noise.

"That CO be trippin' for sure!" Angel announced shaking her head in disbelief. "Never heard anything like it. She got issues for real!" We all knew we just needed to steer clear of her and hope that Mr. Boyd would be back soon!

Early the next morning, I reported to work in the kitchen at my scheduled time. Miss C called me into the office.

"Hey Friend. I hear you will be leaving us soon?"

"Yes ma'am" I answered, grinning slightly.

"Well, you deserve it, but we sure gonna miss you around here. You do a good job and I hate to lose you, but I'm happy for you."

"Thank you Miss C. I really appreciate all that you've done for me as well," I sincerely stated.

It would be another three days in the kitchen, and then I would be ready to start my new job on Monday morning. Meanwhile we learned that Angel had lost her job going to the warehouse, but she would never tell us what happened. She stayed in her bed and cried for two days. I knew I wouldn't be taking her position, but still felt somewhat guilty and awkward now that I would be going out for work, and she would have to stay behind within the compound.

In an attempt to relieve me of my ill feelings, Sofie offered, "Look, you know she done somethin' shady for real, or she wouldn't be so upset. She'd be carryin' on about how unfair it was or sayin' what someone else did to cause her to lose her job. She just got to figure this out on her own. She be okay. You just take care of you right now. You do what you gotta do." I knew she was right.

Early the following Monday morning, we were directed to the intake area, patted down and then boarded onto the van to the event center/warehouse. I acknowledged Helen and Tonya, the "rich" couple who would sometimes play cards with us in the evening - and took a seat behind them in the back of the van.

Helen turned around. "Hey Friend! So, you get to join us in the outside world?" she asked. "Good for you. You need anything at all, you just ask us. You'll like it there."

Soon another inmate joined me in the seat, introduced herself, and then in an attempt to make small talk, asked me how long I had "been down for?" Desiree was an attractive, but rather "chunky" light-skinned black woman, most likely in her late 30's or early 40's. She was nice and friendly, and I was glad to be seated next to her.

"Six months," I answered.

Hesitantly she asked, "You mean six years?"

"No, six months."

"That can't be right. No one gets to go outside of the prison unless you've served at least two years. I never heard of that," she stated questionably. She shared that she had been imprisoned for five years now.

I didn't know what to tell her, but I did know that God just kept opening doors – and gates - for me that should have never been opened. I was in still complete awe of how much He must truly love me. I just could not get over that as horrible as I had been, how He could be so gracious and forgiving of me? *Why God? How could you possibly be so kind to me? I have done nothing to deserve this.*

One of only eight inmates permitted to leave the facility for outside work privileges, I was indeed blessed of the opportunity to drive out of the gated facility; to view the early morning sun glaring across the roads and highways, and watch the cars drive by. As I sat against the window, I observed the people who were possibly going to work or school; maybe shopping or to the bank, or out for breakfast. I was shocked at the price of gasoline. It was now $1.48 per gallon, compared to only .99 when I left for Maryswood in the fall. I gazed at the grass growing along the side of the road, and all I could see was the freedom of God's green earth. Even the dead weeds from the winter months looked beautiful to me! I was *free* – well somewhat.

Arriving at the facility, we entered in through the back gates, were escorted into the shipping docks area, and directed to our various job sites within the warehouse/offices by the CO who brought us in. Before we separated, a final reminder was given to each of us that we were guests at the facility, and to obey all rules that had been given to us previously. No contraband, no smoking, no problems!

As we walked through the warehouse, there were several inmates from a local men's prison that had also been granted outside work privileges. As the cat calls began, I could tell there would somehow be problems with these inmates of the opposite sex. I was eventually escorted to the 2nd floor to the accounting office at the top of the stairs, where I was instructed to wait for the accountant, Miss Bromley to arrive. As I entered a small dark room with no windows; old, faded and tattered furniture and carpeting, I took a seat at one of the office chairs positioned in front of her desk and took note of the silver nameplate located on top of the desk. As an inmate who is never permitted to be left alone without escort, I felt awkward being in this room by myself.

Within a few minutes Miss Bromley entered the room carrying a cup of coffee, abruptly stopped and asked "Who you? No one told me nothin' about having an inmate work with me today. You sure you in the right place?"

I was immediately aware she was not pleased that I was in her office, or that she would be required to work with an inmate. Most likely a "30-something" rather frumpy and unfashionable dark-skinned woman; sporting large black glasses and a sizable backside, she was also stern and bordering on rude.

She picked up the phone and called downstairs to ask someone if I had been assigned to her office, and that certainly there must be a mistake because she had not been made aware of this assignment. After hanging up the phone she continued to complain, although explained "her" rules, expectations and that I was not to ask her any questions, as she was very busy. *So . . . how will I be able to do my job if I can't ask any questions?* But soon enough it was made clear as she ordered me to do several mundane tasks, like counting particular items on a page, adding them up, and then recording them. I sat every quietly at a small table with a single light in the corner and did as I was told. I knew I could do the job, but it was so dull, dark, and depressing. I honestly thought I would almost rather be back in the kitchen at the compound.

Eventually it was lunchtime, and I was directed to the lunch area where I joined the other inmates in the employee kitchen, a large brightly lit room with several tables and chairs. I was introduced to some of the warehouse/office employees who were also given the extra duties of overseeing the inmates. Everyone was talking and laughing, and I realized this was quite a different atmosphere.

"What do you want for lunch Friend? There's lunchmeat, chips, pasta salad and cake. Help yourself," Desiree directed as I headed to the table set up with various sandwiches and side dishes.

"So, what do you think Friend?" Helen proceeded to inquire as I took a seat at the same table with her, Tonya and "Des".

"I don't know. I'm not crazy about the department I've been assigned to. But I guess I still get to work outside and make a little more money. Maybe Miss Bromley will eventually warm up to me." I shrugged my shoulders.

"Bromley? You with Bromley? Oh, Lord girl! No wonder you're discouraged. I worked for her one day. She went on and on about don't touch her purse or her personal stuff. I thought w*oman, I sure don't want your purse! You ain't got nothin' in that purse that I want, that's for sure. You're not rich enough for me to take anything from you! I don't want your piddly little a_ _ money. I want the big stuff. You don't make enough money working here that I want anything from you!*" I recalled that Helen was serving time for grand theft and larceny.

"Well, how'd you get out of there?" I earnestly wanted to know.

"Oh, you won't have to worry. She'll get you out quick enough. She don't like anyone working with her anyhow." She waved off my concern like a fly and changed the subject, proceeding to explain to me about the food in the refrigerator, deep freeze and cupboards that were filled with snacks and drinks provided by the prison.

"And the ladies here are real nice about bringing in cakes, candy & sometimes real homemade food!" Tonya chimed in.

"Yea, but don't be tellin' anyone about that," Helen warned.

"They're really not supposed to do that. They just do it to be nice to us."

I didn't see Des again until after lunch when we went out to sit in rocking chairs on the front porch of the building, where she was smoking with some of the other ladies. "I thought we couldn't smoke here?" I asked Tonya.

"Oh, we not. But no one ever says anything to us. But if they do, it's 'cause someone from the prison or supervisors around, so they warn us to stop!"

As we sat there and watched the traffic go by, I was stunned to realize that we could literally just walk away from this facility if we had wanted! But of course, that would mean "catching" another charge of felony escape and going back to Maryswood for another five to eight years.

After lunch break, I began to make my way back up to the 2nd floor when I heard my name called out. "Friend?"

"Yes ma'am?" I turned and answered one of the staff members. "It seems there has been a mistake and you are actually going to be working in the event department. Follow me," she instructed.

I then remembered that Sergeant Collins had actually told me I would be working in the "event center". This day was certainly full of surprises, and I was delighted! If it meant I didn't have to work in that cramped dingy office with an unpleasant person, then I was pleased enough - but it also meant I would be working in a department of which I was very familiar.

The event center was structured and set-up to perform the work required of exactly what my own business had previously been – a company contracted to work with associations, trade shows and conventions. As with my own firm, we were responsible for preparing packets and folders that would be distributed to the attendees of large annual meetings, conferences and trade shows; sorting and packing boxes with nametags, handouts, brochures, and newsletters that we had created on-sight; as well as whatever else might be necessary for each particular event.

I was in absolute amazement of this assignment. God had placed me right in the middle of the type of work I knew and loved. Although I knew I would never be able to work in this particular field again, I had to wonder again: *how much more could my true Father in heaven love me this much?*

If you, then, though you are evil, know how to give good gifts to your children, how much more will your Father in heaven give good gifts to those who ask him!   *Matthew 7:11*

Chapter 9

❦   *Redemption*   ❧

n: the act, process, or an instance of redeeming; the redemption of his reputation; a sinner's search for redemption. Liberation, recovery, restoration, salvation, deliverance, rescue, release.

"It is because of him that you are in Christ Jesus, who has become for us wisdom from God - that is, our righteousness, holiness and redemption."   1 Corinthians 1:30

. . . and May Flowers

Flowers appear on the earth; the season of singing has come; the cooing of doves is heard in our land. Song of Solomon 2:12

The first day of May. That time of year when the days begin to lengthen, the ground thaws out, the trees bud, the flowers blush, and you are at long last released from the persistent depressive thoughts of the long and cold wintery months. The grass was greener, the flowers along the way to the warehouse each day were infinitely beautiful, and the sun was bright and filled with the warmth of hope.

I relished every moment of freedom, and the ability to leave the compound five days a week. Although required to endure a thorough and humiliating strip search each day upon arrival back inside the prison walls, it was far surpassed by the sheer renewal and liberation within the outside world.

I would lie in my bunk at night and thank God for this gift of freedom that I used to take for granted, and pray He would never ever allow me to forget one of the most valuable assets of my life was indeed my free will - my time, my speech, my home, and my job; but most importantly my freedom to believe in Jesus Christ. I was well aware the prison staff controlled my every movement: when I could go to bed, required to stand at attention; go to work, take a shower, or when I could eat. However, I knew the one thing they could never take away from me was the ability and freedom to control my heart, my mind, and my soul.

I could believe what I chose to believe, feel as I wanted to feel, think as I aspired to think, and speak what I desired to say. I did realize however, that I had reached the crossroad in my life when I had to make serious and deliberate decisions about my future. I alone could determine what my heart, my soul and demeaner would be. I had the freedom to choose to be angry, full of regret, and blame everyone else for all the pain and turmoil in my life; or I could willfully turn my life over to Jesus Christ and give it all – the pain, the deceit, the fear – to Him. I resolved to humble myself and ask for mercy, grace, and forgiveness; to let Him teach me be wise, kind, and forgiving; and to mold me into the woman He had created me to be.

So God said . . . "Since you have asked for this and not for long life or wealth for yourself, nor have asked for the death of your enemies, but for discernment in administering justice, I will do what you have asked. I will give you a wise and discerning heart, so that there will never have been anyone like you, nor will there ever be."   *1 Kings 3:11-12*

Spiritual Raid

Returning back from work that heated Monday afternoon, the passionate balminess of the sun felt invigorating on my skin. I walked the grounds amid the laughter and frolicking of the women, and now at long last, there was joy and good cheer bubbling among the large groups gathered on the green and grassy banks of the yard. Waiting for dinner call, several of the inmates had rolled up the pant legs and short sleeves of their prison khakis in an attempt to absorb as much of the sun enriched rays as they possibly could.

Of course, the COs eventually made their way to the yard and instructed the women to roll down their pant legs and shirt sleeves. It was considered "out of uniform" if the official dress was not worn as they were designed. Regardless, amid a few minor groans of disappointment, the atmosphere and gregarious mood of unreserved delight could not be deterred. Like the spring weather promised, there was faith in new and better days ahead.

A few days later, I entered my room after work and was immediately caught off guard at the sight of my belongings scattered throughout the floor of the cell. None of my bunkies were in the room at the time, so I couldn't ask anyone what had taken place while I was gone. I hurriedly ran next door and asked the one inmate who was in her room what had happened? Had there been a shake-down of the cells that day?

"No. I don't know what could'a happened. There wasn't a shake-down. You sure someone didn't steal your stuff? You know how these *b. . . .s* be shady for real to take your stuff and buy cigarettes. Since no more smoking allowed, these *b. . . . s* be crazy now!"

I knew exactly what she was talking about. The Warden had announced sometime in March that effective May 1st, there would be no more smoking permitted on the premises. All sales of cigarettes had been halted at commissary during the month of April, and any cigarettes confiscated after the effective date, would be considered as contraband. Many of the prisoners who were avid smokers and had any amount of money on their books, had already hoarded all the cigarettes from commissary. The treasured, but forbidden items were then either well-hidden for later consumption, sold for an outrageous price "on the street", or used for alternative payment of "services." Those who were without cigarettes were either pulling and drying grass to be rolled and smoked, or were often breaking into and stealing items from the lock boxes of other inmates to sell for cigarettes. A few others were purposely being caught with the illegal contraband in order to obtain charges, and then transferred back to Maryswood where smoking was still permitted. I truly thanked God this was one habit I had never indulged in.

"Oh, great. I don't know. I guess maybe that's what happened. I better figure out what's gone. Thanks anyhow," I muttered.

Going through all the items I thought I should have in my possession, I was surprised to find that my contacts were missing. Who on earth would want my contacts created with a specific prescription? I realized several other personal items, shampoo, deodorant, razors, and my headset were missing. I was especially upset about the headset because I would often listen to soothing music as I would doze off to sleep at night.

I eventually picked everything up off the floor and replaced the items back in the box as I sorted through and completed a mental inventory list. As I noticed the book *The Bride Wears Combat Boots* I had previously won at Bible Bingo several months earlier, I whispered to myself *that's probably the one item I didn't care if anyone had taken.* I fit it back into the steel box. *Hmm, I guess they weren't thrilled about this book any more than I was?* But then maybe God had other plans for me about that book? Who knew?

Upon completing my checklist of missing objects, I made my way down to the CO's desk to fill out a report of the theft. I was almost done when I spotted Sofie across the room by the library. I motioned for her to come over so we could walk to CFS together for dinner, and I could ask her if she saw or knew anything about what happened.

"Hey girl! Have you been upstairs within the past hour, or have you been working in the library since count time?" I calmly asked her as we headed out the door to the courtyard.

"'Cept for count and right after lunch, I've been down here all day. Why?"

"'Cause somehow somebody broke into my lockbox and stole a bunch of things. I'm not sure of everything that might have been taken, but it seems like quite a few things that now I'm going to have to figure out how to replace when I can. I sure don't know when I can get anymore contacts. It took me forever the first time. I just can't believe that someone would do that to me!"

Wow. Now there was a statement for sure. I, of all people,

couldn't believe that someone would steal something from *me*. And these were all minor items; nothing of real value.

"How you know that someone stole from you?" Sofie inquired.

"What else could it be? 'Ol girl next door said there wasn't a shake down. And you know how crazy all these women have been acting and stealing so they can get cigarettes. It's the only thing it could be. But it's ok. I turned in a report to the CO in case anyone comes up with anything, although I highly doubt that!"

Immediately stopping short in front of the steps to CFS, Sofie turned to face me and grabbed my shoulder. "You did what?! You reported it to the CO? Why would you do that?!" With eyes wide open and almost panic stricken, she confronted me with shock and horror in her voice.

"Yes. Why? I want to get my things back if I can."

"Girl! Do you know what you have done?" as Sofie's dark complexion turned as pale as could be for a black woman.

"No. What's wrong with you?" She was starting to scare me.

"Girl! First of all, you don't *ever* rat out inmates for nothin'! You know what they do to snitches up in here? But *I* took those things to teach you a lesson! You done gone and left again this morning without locking your lockbox! I have told you over and over to lock that box just because of that very thing - that these women be off the hook and stealing from everyone! Why you think you any different? I put everything in my dresser drawer. Oh my God. Now what am I gonna do?" she asked with sincere desperation in her voice.

"Come on! We're going back to the dorm right this minute and you're going to tell Mr. Boyd there's been a mistake and you forgot that you asked me to keep those things safe for you!" she ordered with half-witted confidence.

"Wait! What? What should I say? That doesn't even make any sense. Your drawer isn't locked," I answered, now with fear of my own. We both knew that having possession of anyone else's property, for *any* reason, was punishable with a stay in the "hole".

"I don't know. But you better come up with something 'cause they gonna search our room now for sure and find those things in my drawer and I be goin' to the hole!"

"Sofie. Let's think about this for a minute. I can't say I *asked* you to keep them for me either, or we're both going to the hole!"

"Ok, look. Let's just go back to the room right now and switch everything back before anyone go into our room. If they ask you anything at all, you just say they must have put your things back. Don't even say anything at all to the CO's unless they ask. We just gotta put everything back right now! Don't be actin' funny or nothin'. Just normal."

We calmly turned around and headed back to the dorm. We decided to talk naturally and laugh with each other so the CO wouldn't suspect anything. Regardless, Mr. Boyd stopped us.

"What are you two up to? Not going to dinner?" eyes squinted, with a look of total disbelief and hesitation upon his face.

"Oh. . .yes, but I left a book up in the room I wanted to show her," nodding my head toward Sofie. I had to think quick and the first thing that came to mind was that book I didn't want. "We'll be right back." Oddly enough I thought it was sad that I knew how to lie so quickly and so well.

We scrambled up the open steps to our cell and fell to the floor with pleas of grace and mercy to cover up our deception. "*Oh, God. Please don't let us get into trouble. Sofie was just trying to help me,*" I softly prayed.

We immediately and quietly removed all the missing items from Sofie's dresser drawer and replaced them back in my lockbox, and then set the combination lock. As we began to leave, I suddenly remembered I had locked the book inside the box. I needed to retrieve it before we could return downstairs. We could also hear Mr. Boyd walking throughout the unit, so we hurriedly snatched up the book and quietly re-locked the box.

Once outside, we both heaved a sigh of relief and thanks to God. "You know Sofie. Funny how I worry so much about the supposedly "little" things now. Why couldn't I have figured all that out before being so stupid about the major crimes in my life?"

"God got a plan for you, girl. There ain't nothing in your life that God don't already know about, has a reason for, or provides a way for you. He wants you to learn all of these things, and none of them ain't nothing you can read in no textbook. You gotta live it out girl. The lessons might be hard, but they for real. You don't ever forget them, and you become a better person. You become the person God created you to be."

Sofie had such great wisdom. I already knew the plan God had for her. She was meant to be here in this place for me, and all the other women who turned to her for prayer, direction and insight.

"As a prisoner for the Lord, then, I urge you to live a life worthy of the calling you have received."   *Ephesians 4:1*

The Bride Wears Combat Boots

Later that same evening after returning from the game room and getting things ready for the next day, I started up the ladder of my bunk when I spotted "that" book lying on top of the lockbox. I reached down and picked it up before I crawled up onto my bed. I began to sense that God had placed this in my hands for a reason, so at least I could look through it. Besides, I didn't have any other reading material right then. I glanced again at the front of this rather strange (to me) book title. Who was the "Bride"? And why on earth would she be wearing "Combat Boots?"

I flipped the book over and read the back: *"Get Your Boots On Church!* If you're ready to move past the basics of the faith, this book is for you. If you hunger to be transformed into the image of Christ and not just be busy for God, you've come to the right place. If you're already in the heat of battle and wonder if there is any victory in sight, take heart – it's just over the horizon!"

"In these pages you'll not only find the encouragement to go on, you'll be equipped for victory. You'll learn how to identify the "dark areas of the soul" the enemy uses to infiltrate our thoughts and gain a foothold. . .When the Lord returns for His Bride (the church) will you be MIA, AWOL or a POW? Or will you be pure, but powerful; strong, but sensitive; beautiful but bold; meek, but mighty – prepared for His return?"

I was inspired. I knew I needed victory. It was heavy

on my mind that in less than one month, I would be losing my apartment; Jennifer would have to move in with her sisters, and all of our belongings would be stored in my oldest daughter's barn. I wasn't sure where the next several months were going to take me, or my children. I knew I had no control over any of these things, and desperately needed hope, encouragement and a lot of faith right now. I wasn't sure what this book could teach me, but the message sounded promising. I continued to read the introduction and learned the author was from a hometown only about 30 miles from my home. Ok, I was curious. I needed to read this book.

At that time the kingdom of heaven will be like ten virgins who took their lamps and went out to meet the bridegroom. . . The foolish ones took their lamps but did not take any oil with them. The wise ones, however, took oil in jars along with their lamps. The bridegroom was a long time in coming . . . At midnight the cry rang out: 'Here's the bridegroom! Come out to meet him'. . . But while they (the foolish ones) were on their way to buy oil, the bridegroom arrived. The virgins who were ready went in with him to the wedding banquet. And the door was shut. Later the others also came. 'Lord, Lord,' they said, 'open the door for us!' "But he replied, 'Truly I tell you, I do not know you.' Therefore, keep watch, because you do not know the day or the hour. [Of the return of Jesus] *Matthew 25:1, 3-6, 10-13*

I began to read and absorb the words of that previously unwanted book of great spiritual knowledge and understanding. God was leading me to a new and convicting awareness within my mind and my heart. I began to recognize and grasp the understanding that I needed to be "prepared" for not only whatever God had planned for me in the months and years ahead, but for the predestined return of our Lord and Savior, Jesus Christ.

But about that day or hour no one knows, not even the angels in heaven, nor the Son, but only the Father. As it was in the days of Noah, so it will be at the coming of the Son of Man. For in the days before the flood, people were eating and drinking, marrying and giving in marriage, up to the day Noah entered the ark; and they knew nothing about what would happen until the flood came and took them all away. That is how it will be at the coming of the Son of Man. . .Therefore keep watch, because you do not know on what day your Lord will come. But understand this: If the owner of the house had known at what time of night the thief was coming, he would have kept watch and would not have let his house be broken into. So you also must be ready, because the Son of Man will come at an hour when you do not expect him."

Matthew 24:36-39 & 42-44

The Final Walk

. . . for I know that through your prayers and God's provision of the Spirit of Jesus Christ, what has happened to me will turn out for my deliverance. *Philippians 1:19*

"Friend. Get up. You have to report downstairs for escort to the Admin building. Come on, get up," Ms. Crothers, the night CO quietly advised me. With a flashlight held directly above my head, Ms. Crothers informed me again that I would need to get up, get dressed and report downstairs to her desk for escort to the campus area.

"Yes Ma'am. What time is it?" I whispered, trying to adjust my eyes to the extremely dark hour of the morning.

"About 4:00 am. Come on. Get up now. I'll see you downstairs."

"Yes Ma'am."

I awkwardly attempted to quietly climb down the ladder and get dressed without stirring anyone. I had to wonder what this unsettling scenario could possibly mean?

It was Tuesday, May 9th. I remembered because this was my Dad's birthday. I would have to make sure to call him when I returned from work that afternoon.

I soon made my way downstairs to the CO cubicle, where I recognized Tonya and Helen already standing at the desk.

"Hey ladies. What's going on? Why are we down here?" I softly inquired.

"Oh, Lord. Who knows?" Helen answered. "But one thing for sure now that we see you, it gotta be something about working at the warehouse," she replied in a similar murmur.

As the grounds CO came inside the door to escort us to our destination, we soon realized that indeed, everyone who worked at the warehouse had already been tagged at their unit.

Immediately the speculations and the whispers initiated among the women. "Look, don't no one say NOTHIING 'bout smoking at the warehouse, or getting food, candy, snacks or birthday cakes from the workers! We'll all lose our jobs!"

There had also been rumors often discussed in the van between the inmates regarding the men and women who were sneaking through the vents in the ceilings to "spend time" together, as well as to get cigarettes from the guys who were allowed to have them. Several weeks earlier I learned this was allegedly the reason Angel had lost her job at the warehouse. But I never confronted her about it. I knew she wasn't a smoker, and I could only speculate what else she might have been up to with the guys from the men's prison.

"Alright ladies. Take a seat. The officers will be with you shortly," we were instructed. We took our seats on the long wooden benches: the same benches where we waited to go before the parole board. I concluded these were most certainly the "hot seats".

"There will be no talking among you. You will be called in one at a time for questioning. You will return to your seat after interrogation for further instructions."

Interrogation? I was not thrilled with this process at all! Several "knowingly" and deliberate glares commenced between the inmates, silently commanding "you *know* what NOT to say!"

One by one, called into the "interview/court" room, we were asked questions regarding smoking, interaction with the men, or any unauthorized parties or food provided. I truthfully did not know anything about how the women were getting cigarettes, or somehow smuggling them back inside the compound; nor if or how anyone might be meeting up with the men. Of course, I had overheard the rumors and had my suspicions, but I did not know anything that was factual or who might be involved. Therefore, I honestly stated that I did not know anything about those things. They never asked me if I ever saw anyone smoking on the grounds. That was a different scenario in my mind.

But I struggled with the party question. When asked, I had to confess there were a few times there may have been some cake, but that I honestly did not know where it may have come from. I was waiting for the hatchet to fall! Were we all going to lose our jobs, and/or would the staff at the warehouse get fired now? I was dismissed and left the room with a heavy heart. I took my place back on the bench with a look of despair and worry - not one of boldness or audacity. Maybe that was a "tell-tale" sign of sorts.

Once we completed the cross-examination, we were instructed that we could either go to CFS for breakfast or return to our cells; but we were not to be anyplace else on the compound. This was in order that we could be reached if necessary to be called back in for further questioning.

I usually didn't go to breakfast before work; however, I was already up and still had well over an hour before we would be called to report to the Admissions area for transport. Or would we even be going out today? I barely tasted the food on my plate, wondering what would happen this day?

As I departed down the steps of CFS on my way back to my unit, an inmate approached me and asked, "Where you been?!" Mr. Boyd lookin' for you!"

"What? I went to breakfast. They said we could go to CFS." I stumbled over my words. I thought certainly I was in trouble now.

"Well, I don't know 'bout all that, but I do know he want you right now!"

I scurried over to my unit and promptly entered the atrium area where Mr. Boyd was seated at his desk.

"Mr. Boyd, I promise you they told us we could go to CFS. I was right where they said we could go. I'm sorry." I blurted out in fear that he would write me up.

"Friend? I don't know what you're talking about. What I do know is that you have ten minutes to gather your things and report to Intake, or you're not going anywhere! You're scheduled to go out today," he shared with a half-grin.

"What?" I was completely confused. "Where am I going?"

"Did I stutter? Do you want to go home today or not? Now *git* or you're not going anyplace!" he half laughed, half shouted.

I couldn't help myself. "Home? You mean *home* – like to *my* home?" I was in total shock.

"Yes, now GO! They're waiting for you!" he reiterated.

"Yes sir!" It didn't take any more convincing. But I certainly didn't understand. I still had five months to serve. I immediately ran up the stairs and into our room. Sofie was still in her bed.

"Sofie, you awake?"

"Well, I been trying to sleep, but everyone up in here lookin' for you! Where you been anyhow?"

"You gotta wake up! I'm going home today! I don't know how or why, but Mr. Boyd said I'm going home!"

Sofie bolted up out of the bed. "You're going home? Oh my! Ok, well what can I do to help you? You gotta get your things together!"

"I know. Mr. Boyd said I have 10 minutes. I'm hurrying,"

as I quickly gathered up everything I personally owned and stuffed into my laundry bag.

"Here, you gonna need a basket to carry all of your state things over to turn in at Intake. I'll go downstairs and get one for you," she declared as she swiftly pulled on her scrubs and new tennis shoes to go to the laundry room. I was happy, and yet couldn't help but feel sad for Sofie who had been waiting over 10 years now. She still had two years yet to serve.

Angel had already left for work at CFS that morning, and Joy was up and getting ready for the day, as well. "Good luck to you Friend. I hope everything works out for you. Don't be gettin' in anymore trouble now!" she advised.

"Thanks Joy. You do the same. Hope your time goes fast and you get back home to those boys soon!" I reached up and gave her a quick hug before she left the room.

My mind was whirling with so many questions and possible assumptions of what could have taken place that I would now be permitted to go home. But deep inside, I knew that God had His hand in it.

Now the Lord is the Spirit, and where the Spirit of the Lord is, there is freedom.　　　　*2ⁿᵈ Corinthians 3:17*

Sofie came back with a tall clothes basket and started dumping my "institutional" clothes, sheets, blankets, boots and other items from my small closet and dresser drawer. She helped me carry everything downstairs and asked Mr. Boyd if she could assist me to transfer my things.

"Yep. I'll let Intake know you're on your way. Good luck Friend. And don't let me see you back in here again!"

he genuinely offered as he spun around in his seat to reach for the phone.

"No sir, I won't. Thank you!"

Sofie and I carried everything over to Intake and began the process of inventory as all state-issued items must be accounted for. Finally, all personal items must also be itemized and stored into a box for later shipping or pick-up. I would not be permitted to carry anything outside of the prison walls with me.

"You good to go Friend. Be careful out there girl," the Intake officer extended her wishes of good luck.

Sofie and I slowly moved into the hallway as I would now report to Admissions and Sofie would return to the unit. I tried to hold back the tears as I held her tightly, gently kissed her on the cheek and offered my sincere gratitude for all that she had provided to me.

"Now, stop that girl! You know everyone up in here be thinkin' we carryin' on or something!" as she firmly hugged me right back and laughed. We both shed a few tears and promised to stay in touch.

"Sofie, I will never forget you. I promise I will write you as soon as I get home and know where I'm going to be. I'll get you a phone number so you can call me. I know I can't come back in to visit with you, but we'll stay in touch for real."

We then parted our ways and I headed to the Admissions area.

Upon entrance to Admissions, I approached the desk with great apprehension and fear . . . fear that this would only prove to be a misunderstanding, and that I would be required to return to my unit after all. Eventually ordered to take a seat just outside the office, I was to wait there until an officer from my county jail arrived to pick me up. Relieved to hear those words, I was thankful to be moving forward one more step in the process.

As I took my seat, and overtly aware that the chairs and benches for the inmates were always hard and cold, memories of those who would tell me, *"Friend, you forget where you are girl! You the prisoner!"* would come to mind. I chuckled to myself as I thanked God for this unbelievable miracle and was grateful to be sitting on a cold hard bench waiting to be released!

Still in disbelief of the situation and afraid to believe this could be happening, my mind continued to search for possibilities regarding this outcome. I recalled I had written a letter to my attorney Katherine, sometime in March regarding the likelihood of early Judicial Release. I did receive a response from her indicating that she would forward my request to the Judge; however, I would have to wait the required time frame of six months and could not submit the appeal until the end of April (This was May 9th). She also explained that she would request letters from various family members and friends regarding my usual character, values, and integrity. Regardless, she clearly stated all of this could take several weeks or even months; but more importantly - not to expect a positive response to my request. The judge had been very clear in his statement that I must serve my full year.

I concluded the judge had not released me. There must be some problem with my case. I knew of a few women who were called back to their county jail, thinking they were going home; only to find out they were ordered back regarding something inaccurate with their paperwork, or specifically with their case that must be reinstated in front of a judge. I was convinced this must be the reason.

Eventually 8:00 am came and went, and the ladies who would have normally been escorted through Admissions to report for work at the warehouse, never came through. I realized no one would be going outside the compound today. I had to wonder what was going on with that whole situation, and what the outcome would be. I waited a few more hours, and eventually checked back at the desk to see if I could use the bathroom, as well as to question if there might be any word about the time frame regarding the deputy from my county?

"Friend, they'll be here. Don't worry. Hold on and we'll be right with you," the CO responded, as someone would have to escort me to the bathroom.

"Come on, I'll take you," the attending CO stated as she motioned for me to follow her to the restroom, and then asked "So, you're going out today?"

"I sure hope so," I answered more of a questionable statement rather than a positive note.

On the way back to the bench she reassured me, "Don't worry. They'll be here soon. Good luck out there."

As I returned to my seat, I recognized two of the corporate officers who had questioned me earlier that morning regarding the warehouse, walking through the solid metal doors into the Admissions area. They were casually talking to each other, and as we made eye contact, one of them stopped and asked if I had been in the interrogation room earlier that morning?

"Yes sir," I hesitantly answered.

"No one is going out today. Are you here for another reason?"

"Yes sir. I'm going back to my county today," I blurted out, so pleased to be able to say those words; and yet my heart skipping a beat as I now worried that I would be detained.

"Ok. I'm thinking we may want to speak with you again before you leave," as he looked to the other officer as if to confirm that they should question me further. "Just a minute while we let someone know where you will be."

"Yes sir." I wasn't quite sure I liked this additional delay, although pleased he did say I would be right back.

"Ok, we're going over to the Captain's office. We may need to take a few more statements."

I got up and followed them out of the doors. I knew I would have to make my way back across campus to reach the Officer's unit. I really did *not* want to make that walk back into the general compound. I had been on my way out of the prison, and now felt as though something might happen that would forbid me to leave.

As we trekked the long circular cement sidewalk leading to the unit, I could hear several of the inmates talking about me throughout the entire courtyard. Not quite sure what they might be saying, I didn't even look up. And then it was very clear:

"SNITCH! I told y'all she was a snitch! What did I tell you? Didn't I say she was nothing but a liar and a snitch? There she go, ratting everyone out and now everyone be losin' they job! Hey Friend! You goin' down *b...h*!"

Stopping in my tracks, and gasping for air, I immediately recognized Bowman's voice. Several others joined in with her jeering and taunting of me. From clear across the yard, Bowman was letting the entire inmate population know that she was calling me out.

"Come on. Don't pay attention to them. You're going out today," the officer consoled me. Then he tracked down a CO to take Bowman into custody. But it was too late. The damage was done. I prayed to God that I *had* to go home now. I would not be able to come back here. Although it was all a lie, it wouldn't matter. The word was out on me now. Thoughts of my previous dreadful altercations with Peaches at Maryswood filled my mind. I was reliving the fear of possibly being violently attacked, going to the hole for protection, or losing my standing with others knowing they could interact with me without fear of repercussions.

Oh, God. Please let me go home today!

At that moment, I reflected on the injustice and undeserved violence Jesus suffered (although I would nowhere near, nor *ever* experience the degree of which He endured) as He was dragged through the streets, tormented and taunted by the crowd. I hung my head as I realized that although everything the Jewish people had said about Jesus were lies, it wouldn't matter. He was to be convicted. The officer of the high court, Pontius Pilate the governor, had attempted to spare Jesus by offering up an alternative to the people - another prisoner, a convicted murderer, to take the punishment (to be hung on the cross until death) - but it would be to no avail. The people had spoken.

Then the governor's soldiers took Jesus into the Praetorium [courtyard] *and gathered the whole company of soldiers around him. They stripped him and put a scarlet robe on him, and then twisted together a crown of thorns and set it on his head. They put a staff in his right hand. Then they knelt in front of him and mocked him. "Hail, king of the Jews!" they said. They spit on him and took the staff and struck him on the head again and again. After they had mocked him, they took off the robe and put his own clothes on him. Then they led him away to crucify him."*   *Matthew 27:27-31*

And yet, in spite of these circumstances and the uncertainty of my future, I knew the promises of God were real. He had made Himself known to me over and over. Walking through the courtyard and crowd of mockers revealed to me a new definition of faith: I could absolutely trust this Jesus who loved me like that, no matter what else might happen to me.

Then I knew: ***this is faith***.

"Though he slay me, yet will I hope in him; I will surely defend my ways to his face."   *Job 13:15*

EPILOGUE

n. a concluding section that rounds out the design of a literary work; a speech often in verse addressed to the audience by an actor at the end of a play; the final scene of a play that comments on or summarizes the main action; the concluding section of a musical composition.

There are 458 times the word ***faith*** is used in the Bible. The word itself can have many different meanings and be used in different situations.

*Then Jesus said to her, "Woman, you have great **faith**! Your request is granted." And her daughter was healed at that moment.*   *Matthew 15:28*

*Consequently, **faith** comes from hearing the message, and the message is heard through the word about Christ.*
Romans 10:17

In Chapter 6, I explained how I realized I had faith, but it was often in material things: my boyfriend, my home, my ability to earn income, in myself. In prison I learned I could not put my faith in the system, other people, my income, but especially within myself.

I have recently noticed a lot of *Life Coaches* advising of self-help, self-love, and self-acceptance exercises and techniques of *who we are* (within ourselves) in a lot of different women's groups on social media. *Not* at all to say that these beliefs or feelings we have of ourselves, or other people/circumstances are not beneficial in order for us to have strong relationships, as well as to be physically and mentally healthy. But it *is* unhealthy to believe that **we** have absolute control, faith and final power over everything in our life. How many times has that faith in others, things, or within ourselves sadly ended in profound disappointment or failure? That is because we are human, imperfect and limited in so many ways. But God is eternal and perfect in every way, and we are made right in His eyes by faith alone. As Christians, we have trust/faith in the death of Christ to atone for our sins.

It is also critical to explain our faith needs to be in God as revealed in His Word (Bible), the Truth. Otherwise, we become lost in believing all kinds of false ideas heard from false teachers or profits who claim to represent God. So, we are obligated to test everything we hear by diligent study of the Bible.

Do you understand that we were created by God, for Him, and in His image, but we are truly nothing without Him? We cannot exist without God. On our own, we cannot breathe the air, the blood to flow through our heart, or obtain the gravity that keeps us from floating off into the sky forever, without Him.

*For by grace you have been saved through **faith**. And this is not your own doing; it is the gift of God…   Ephesians 2:8*

Until the onset of COVID-19, I visited the local jail almost every week as I served in a ministry to bring the message of *faith* to women who had lost faith in God, themselves, other people. . . the substance of things hoped for, the evidence of things not seen! My sincere desire in revealing my story is that these women/*you* will discover that God *is* real. He is the same God today that He has always been. He only wants us to come to Him . . . and trust Him. He has a plan and a promise for the very least of us, if only we will follow Him.

By now, you have realized this is still not the "rest of the story". You've been left wondering what happens next, and I know you are not happy with me! For this, I am truly sorry, but there is so *much more* to the story, and many more miracles that I could not fit into this one book alone - so I will share those with you in my next book **Defining Hope**. What takes place in the months after this volume's story will leave you just as captivated, just as hungry for the many accounts of what God does for His children even when all looks hopeless. You will meet several other characters and their lives of crime, drug addiction, prison time, and continued search for a better life. You will be left seeking more adventure, enlightenment and faith for what God has to offer *you*.

So in Christ Jesus you are all children of God through faith, for all of you who were baptized into Christ have clothed yourselves with Christ. There is neither Jew nor Gentile, neither slave nor free, nor is there male and female, for you are all one in Christ Jesus.   Galatians 3:26-28

"**Faith** *goes up the stairs that love built and looks out the windows which* **hope** *has opened."*   Charles Spurgeon

❧ Acknowledgements ❧

n. the act of acknowledging or state of being acknowledged. Something done or given as an expression of thanks or appreciation, as a reply to a message, etc. Recognition of existence or truth of something.

For the continued prayers, encouragement, understanding and love, I wish to thank and acknowledge:

** Always first and foremost to my Father God, my Savior Jesus Christ and most wonderful Holy Spirit who dwells within my heart and soul. Thank you for healing, for placing the dreams to share within my heart, for the true desire to awaken in the very early hours of each morning to write, and the unwavering determination to share this story ~ **Your** story of faith and love.*

** My family for their continued love, support, and reassurance. Through the years I had never stopped dreaming of or praying for a time that we would be free of pain, of tireless struggles, or the evils within our lives. I have since learned that will never happen in **this** lifetime. But I do know we have an unconditional love and devotion to one another - and have Jesus Christ who loves us, comforts us, and through salvation will allow us to be together in heaven together for eternity!*

* My devoted editor, friend and Sister-in-Christ, Janet Maxim. For the countless hours spent editing, counseling and encouraging me through every page of this manuscript. I cannot begin to thank you enough for your continued validation, hard work, and love on this journey we have traveled together.

* The amazing women of God in my prayer and bible

study groups who have prayed for, encouraged, prepared food, provided medical equipment and transportation, cleaned my house, financially helped me with much needed tests, and undeniably supported and loved me through each and every day of the past two years. There has never been a time that I have ever had to question if I could turn to and count on any one of them to reach out to me regarding some portion of my life. I am forever grateful for the strength, resilience and genuine conviction of these women of faith. To: Kathy, Janet, Cat, Christina, Tia, Sue, Vicki, Val, Janice, Lael, Carmen, Linda, and Brenda - I thank, cherish, and love each and every one of you!

I have also been especially grateful for their open willingness to bare their souls, their pain and their strong faith in God despite the tragedies, hopelessness or just everyday trials of their own lives. I have recently been humbled by many of the stories of faith and courage of these women of God. As I have delved into my own pain, my own revelation of what faith is, many have unknowingly inspired a spirit within me that has lifted me up and given me inspiration that God's faith is everlasting!

I recently inquired of these ladies if they might be willing to share their stories with you in the hope it might help and encourage you, as they did for me. This was their loving and overwhelming response:

❧ Testimonies of Faith ❧

n. a solemn declaration usually made orally by a witness under oath in response to a lawyer or authorized public official: firsthand authentication of a fact: evidence: an outward sign: an open acknowledgment: a public profession of religious experience.

"What you heard from me, keep as the pattern of sound teaching, with faith and love in Christ Jesus." Timothy 1:13

Sue's faith in God grew throughout her twenties and early thirties as God took her desire to get married and redirected that desire toward Him. As she grew in her attempted contentment with God alone, and faced the fact that she might never marry, she learned to trust that the Lord was looking out for her best interest similar to how Abraham trusted God when he was asked to sacrifice his son, Isaac, on the altar (Genesis 22:1-19), or how Sarah, by faith, was enabled to bear a child as an old woman (Hebrew 11:11).

As Sue watched all her friends marry, as well as her younger sister, she determined to continue to trust that God loved her and had a plan for her life. It wasn't until Sue was 33 that the Lord had all the pieces in place, and would now bring her together with the husband He had chosen for her. Her continued prayers and devotion to her Father in heaven, would not only be answered, but God would surprise her with the blessing of four small children, all under five-years-old, by the time she was 39. Throughout all the joys, albeit hardships, of caring for and raising her family, she found that her strong faith was in her everyday commitment to God, to her husband, and to her children. Sue states: "What we fail to realize is that of all the mighty men and women we read about [in the Bible] and want to emulate [match, imitate, follow] became who they were through those moment-by-moment acts of faithfulness to God."

* * * * * * * * * * * *

Although never her initial intent for such a large family, *Vicki* was blessed with seven wonderful children: Six boys and one twin girl. She and her husband of several years were devout Christians, playing and singing worship music at their local church throughout the years. They were the perfect example of a loving and faithful marriage.

In 2001, Vicki became more than devasted at the tragic loss of their beloved son, Jordan (son #3), due to a horrific car accident at the age of 21 years. She didn't know how she could possibly get through this turbulent time. A few years later, her husband, her rock, her forever love and provider of 33 years, announced he was leaving the marriage. Once again, Vicki found herself overcome and shattered with so much agony, she described it as being "blind with pain". Distraught and broken, Vicki ran to a faithful family within her church that lovingly took her in and offered the time and space (she describes as the *sanctuary* that God provided) necessary for her to cry, pray and heal. After a few months and hoping that her husband would now realize that he wanted to make the marriage work, Vicki was paralyzed with his rejection and dismissal of their many years together.

In 2010, her only daughter, Amy (#4) would suffer

traumatic mental and physical pain, leaving her beautiful face scarred for life, after a horrific motorcycle accident. During all this time, Vicki clung to her faith as eventually each and every one of the remaining (5) boys would at some point in their life serve time in prison (some previously and others currently in jail), homeless and/or addicted to drugs to this day. Despite her pain and many hardships, Vicki continues her strong faith and prayers for her children. She is blessed when they call upon her for prayers of wisdom, successful recovery from addictions, loneliness, or feelings of failure. Vicki shares that she has:

"Faith in God's Word that is like a two-edged sword. I want to say to that for other mothers who experience their children in jail, please know that Reuben (her youngest - #7) told me to realize that even though the boys went through such strong addictions, they STILL shared the Lord with people that may have never listened to, or heard it from anyone else, because of where they were (prison/on the streets). They were still able to bring some light into the darkness of the drug world. My dream, of course, was that my children would be raised up to share the Lord, but I didn't know it would be in the shadows of their addictions. I feel like they were taught the Way, and that mothers shouldn't give up hope that their children will keep it in their hearts." *Bring up a child in the way he should go.......*" [Refer to Ephesians 6:4]

Vicki's children continue to reach out and are truly seeking the wisdom and strength of an almighty God that is ever present within the heart of their mother. Now happily remarried, Vicki states that it is only through her strong faith that her hope is never ending, and that her belief in the promises of God are real!

* * * * * * * * * * * *

Suffering through a mentally and physically abusive marriage for several years, *Tia* often feared for her life during this time. She would eventually muster up the courage and the money needed to leave this violent relationship, forcing her to become a single, struggling mother to her two young girls, 5 and 10-years old at the time.

It would only be within several months that her struggles would continue. Tia had contracted a life-threatening staph infection throughout her entire body, that would ultimately take one of her legs, causing everything in her life to change again - forever. Tia states that "Faith is knowing that even when someone you love tries to take your life, or sickness and infection takes over your body, that God is the only one that is ALWAYS there, holding your hand and helping you through. Sometimes even if you don't always believe it or deserve it, He's got your back!"

* * * * * * * * * * * *

Val has been a mighty prayer warrior for her family through the years as she and her husband would experience horrific pain and suffering when several heart-rendering events occurred all at the same time. Their oldest daughter succumbed to peer pressure of using drugs while still in High School, and after many court hearings, Renee would be sentenced to a detention home for girls for 30-days, and then required to wear an ankle monitor. Their second daughter, Christina, who was in grade school at the time, developed a heart condition causing many episodes of palpitations and excessive illness. She missed a lot of school and was taken to several heart specialists for many tests. For some unknown reason, the doctors failed to find anything wrong with her heart. Regardless, due to all the time missed, the schools believed that Christina was possibly only faking her illness, and therefore, the system turned Val and her husband Richard in for neglect, and wanted to have their young daughter taken away from them. They were devastated and forced to hire an attorney. Meanwhile Richard lost his job, and they were left no choice other than to file bankruptcy to save their home. Val worked long hours at night and on the weekends to make up for the time and work missed for court and attorney visits, as well as to provide income to the family.

Val shared "I was at my lowest of lows during this time. I prayed harder than I have ever prayed before. We continued to have Faith in God, for his support and holding us above water. The end result was that God answered our prayers in due time! After Renee successfully completed a mandatory out-patient drug program, she graduated and today is a Certified Oncology Nurse, married and has three beautiful children. Christina ended up doing much better in school and was permitted to stay in the home with us. She is now a medical assistant and licensed Massage Therapist, thrilled to learn she had made the Dean's list! Currently engaged to her fiancé of 13 years, they have one child. Richard ended up getting another job and we were able to keep our home. During this time, the stress seemed unbearable. I really feel I wouldn't have been able to get through this time without my faith in the Lord. I still don't know how we did it. He is truly an amazing God!

To me Faith is never giving up no matter what the obstacles are and thanking God in the middle of your trials and dark times. He does not give up on us, so we should never give up on him."

* * * * * * * * * * * *

Experiencing great heartache and facing several challenging and life-changing circumstances throughout her life, *Cat* has maintained her never-ending faith and belief in an amazing and loving God.

Cathy states that her most impressionable pictures of faith are found in the Bible. In Acts 16:22-26, when Paul and Silas are thrown into a cold, dark, jail cell after being beaten and bound in stocks and chains, they choose to start praying and worshipping God in the midst of their suffering. What Cathy loves most about this story is that God proves Himself faithful to these men. In the midst of their praise the prison bars burst open, and the captives go free! The prison guard and his entire family then become believers of Jesus Christ!

The other story is in the book of Job: Job suffers through many horrific losses, and experiences much pain and suffering, although later displays total surrender to God. Job humbles himself and proclaims:

"Though he slay me yet will I trust him". Job 13:15

And at the end of Job's story in Chapter 42, God blesses him with twice as much as he had prior in his life.

The LORD blessed the latter part of Job's life more than the former part. Job 42:12

Cat shares she can only hope to navigate through all of her trials and tribulations of life the way these men of God chose to do, as well as to continue to try to reach souls for God's Kingdom even in the midst of troublesome circumstances. Her life verse is found in Romans 8:28: *And we know that ALL THINGS work together for good to them that love God, to them who are the called according to his purpose.*

Cat states that the word "Faith" is a verb, therefore it is an action word. Trust is also an action verb, consequently Cathy chooses to trust God no matter how long or dark the way may seem - because she believes her God is always faithful - even when she can't always see the way He is taking. He has always been there for and with her.

* * * * * * * * * * *

Over thirty years ago when *Lael* was married, she had a message printed on the wedding program to their guests, asking them to pray for her and her husband - that God would show them how to have the kind of faith expressed in Michael Card's song:

That's What Faith Must Be [5]

To hear with my heart
To see with my soul
To be guided by a hand I cannot hold
To trust in a way that I cannot see
That's what Faith must be.

---

[5] *Michael Card*

Little did she know the journey that God would take them on throughout their marriage, often testing their faith. Over the years, this would include infertility, adoption, her husband's health crisis, financial instability for years after the loss of her husband's job of over 20+ years; and most recently, surgery for Lael for breast cancer.

Lael shares that her faith wavered as her son continued to grow older, and his behavior worsened with each year that passed. God remained silent on prayers to change her son's ways. She became more rebellious toward God. *Who needs a God who refuses to answer your prayers*, she thought? It would be years later, however, that God did speak directly to Lael's heart about her son. Yet, still her faith seemed lukewarm at best.

When Lael received the news of breast cancer, she repented of her rebellious attitude, and began to seek God again. She knew that without a strong faith in God, this new journey would be extremely difficult. She could not know how difficult it would be.

When she learned that her diagnosis was far more serious than she originally thought, it brought fear: fear of the unknown, and fear of death. Lael asked God to draw her closer and to stand by her through these difficult trials, but she was still learning to trust Him - she was still filled with fear.

Lael shared "Fear would come at night when I couldn't sleep, or early in the morning when I first awoke. And although my husband would always pray with me, and encourage me, I realized I needed a way to get through the fear once and for all. One night I was so fearful and afraid of dying that nothing I did helped. I finally realized that I couldn't change the plans that God had for me. If it was His will that this was how I was going to die, then I had to accept that. I confessed to Him that I didn't want to die this young, but if that was His will for my life, then help me to accept it. I prayed, surrendering my life to Him. And just like that, the fear was replaced with peace."

During this time of learning to trust God again, Lael was reading the familiar passage of Proverbs 3:56: *Trust in the Lord with all your heart and lean not on your own understanding. In all your ways **submit** to Him, and He will make your paths straight.* She had never read these verses in the New International Version of the Bible, and now realized the word "acknowledge" had been replaced with the word "submit". She understood what God was showing her: "In all your ways 'yield, resign, or surrender to the power, will or authority of the Lord' - and He will make your paths straight." Lael stated "I know when I trust Him, and have faith in Him, He will make *my* paths straight. I am trying to learn to yield to Him daily, then whenever He should decide to take me from this world, I will not be afraid."

Lael understands that true faith is according to Hebrews 11:1, which says "Now faith is being sure of what we hope for and certain of what we do not see." She continues to share, "We don't always know what God's plans are for our lives, including how many days of life we will have. There are many promises in the Bible that tell us that God will never leave us or forsake us, but that doesn't mean that we will always have a favorable outcome from our trials this side of Heaven. God knows what is best for us, and whatever happens, if we trust Him, He will get the glory and walk us through life every step of the way."

"*Faith* doesn't always take you out of the problem, *Faith* takes you through the problem. *Faith* doesn't always take away the pain, *Faith* gives you the ability to handle the pain. *Faith* doesn't always take you out of the storm, *Faith* calms you in the midst of the storm." – Author Unknown

* * * * * * * * * * * *

I hope you have truly savored these amazing testimonies of *faith.* I strongly encourage you to look deep within your heart and possibly you will find your own story of courage, conviction and *faith!*

Consequently, faith comes from hearing the message, and the message is heard through the word about Christ.

Romans 10:17

Printed in the United States
by Baker & Taylor Publisher Services